THE MUSEUM OF LOST AND FRAGILE THINGS

A Year of Salvage

SUZANNE JOINSON

THE
INDIGO
PRESS

THE INDIGO PRESS
50 Albemarle Street
London W I S 4BD
www.theindigopress.com

The Indigo Press Publishing Limited Reg. No. 10995574
Registered Office: Wellesley House, Duke of Wellington Avenue
Royal Arsenal, London SE18 6SS

First published in Great Britain in 2024 by The Indigo Press

Suzanne Joinson asserts the moral right to be identified as the author of this
work in accordance with the Copyright, Designs and Patents Act 1988

A CIP catalogue record for this book is available from the British Library

ISBN: 978-1-911-648680
eBook ISBN: 978-1-911-648796

Cover design © Luke Bird
Art direction by House of Thought
Author photo © Ben Nicholls
Typeset by Tetragon, London
Printed and bound in Great Britain by TJ Books Limited, Padstow

MIX
Paper | Supporting
responsible forestry
FSC
www.fsc.org   FSC® C013056

DISCLAIMER

This memoir is a work of non-fiction based on my life, written from my perspective. I have drawn on personal memory and family conversations to make sense of my past while fully aware that memory is inevitably subject to error. I have changed names and identifying features to protect privacy in some cases. I acknowledge that there are different viewpoints, and I respect them. My deepest thanks to my family – John, Lynda and David Joinson – for reading and agreeing to the publication of this memoir. We have come through much and remain close, and this means the world to me.

For John, Lynda and David Joinson,
with all my love.

What I'm looking for is the inconsistency of memory, how it stumbles slightly among objects. It's a gesture, or just an intention that asserts itself over the material.

Nathalie Léger, *Exposition*,
translated by Amanda DeMarco

I've written a good deal about the members of my family ... I skirted around them, skirted around all these things...

Marguerite Duras, *The Lover*,
translated by Barbara Bray

Damn it I write things down, ruffle pages and smooth the pillowcases of my mind.

Francesca Woodman, 'Notebook III', 1975

CONTENTS

SUMMER

Ashram is a shelter – provided by Guru Maharaj Ji, unto which we can come, unto which Guru Maharaj Ji can really work at us, really operate at us, really because he is the surgeon, and he knows what's wrong.

Maharaj Ji (Prem Rawat),
Atlantic City conference, 20 December 1976

Paperweight

Perhaps because I'd lost everything, I had an idea that I wanted to create a museum. Or rather, an exhibition of my family. I suppose I thought it would save us. (I was at the point where I would try anything.)

My parents were members of the Divine Light Mission, which is now known as a cult. They grew up in the northern factory town of Crewe, where everyone sawed metal for Rolls-Royce or hammered bits of trains for Crewe Works. That or went blind hemming suits for Chester Barrie. Girls like my mum, who didn't finish school, were routinely shunted towards this large clothes manufacturer. Mum told us that her bad dreams started after a teacher suggested Chester Barrie. Coffins. Open mouths. An endless pit that she was always about to fall into. 'I'd rather die than go and work in Chester Barrie,' she told us, always inclined to the Gothic and dramatic.

Guru Maharaj Ji offered kids of factory towns like Crewe a way out of the industrial grind and a fast track to enlightenment, or what he called Knowledge. His Sony cassette tapes blasted out of our kitchen all day.

All that is material will perish!
Perish! Perish! Perish!
Perfect KNOWLEDGE, not the stuff of life!

Materialism was evil and wages went to the mission. Careers or personal ambitions were meaningless. Stuff, things, objects and matter were all part of the degeneration of civilization (Kali Yuga) and needed to be eradicated. The devoted were to meditate for a minimum of two hours a day, preferably more. If possible, the devoted were always to be in a state of meditation. Sacrifices had to be made; family time was not important. Children were to be put aside; meditation was always the priority. What strikes me now, as I think about my mum shy and pregnant with me at nineteen, is how easy it must have been for Guruji brainwashers to scoop up my parents. How ripe they were for something, anything, that would get them away from the industrial rust and spit of Chester Barrie and Crewe Works.

Four people. Mum, Dad, brother, me. When I was a kid, I believed I could rescue us all. Perhaps I still do.

I was at a car boot sale when it occurred to me that a family is a group of people living with a pile of stuff inside a house. Maybe, then, I could mend a broken family by replacing the things we had lost. I cruised the car boot stalls looking for something, but I didn't know what. My kids and husband had wandered off into the hot, end-of-summer day.

'There's always a paperweight, isn't there?' a woman said as I picked up a glob of glass with a tacky blue dolphin floating inside. She was wiry and wore an oversized plaid shirt and a baseball cap. She sipped from her flask. The word SALVAGERS across the side of her vehicle made me think of cargo strewn on a beach after a wreck. She was so at home in this field that I was tempted to curtsy at her impressive sense of belonging.

'I guess so,' I said. The blue in the glass paperweight was a blue I had seen before. As I held it up to the light, a memory came in so strong I could taste it: a shoebox full of photographs with a paperweight in it much like this one. My dad was plucking individual photographs out, looking at them, then dropping them into a fire he'd lit in a corrugated bin. An *agya* had come through (an instruction) that all things made of paper must be destroyed.

Nineteen eighty-something. Dusk coming in. We were in the back garden of our council house. Dad, Dave, me and the dog scratching his fleas. Mum away in the kitchen. Midges in the air, the low threat of clouds, and our broken swing hanging limp on one chain.

'Don't look so sad, Suzy-Sue,' Dad said, sucking on a rollie. 'It's just paper and dust. Let it all go. It doesn't change how we feel inside.'

He'd been told to destroy anything with Guruji's face looking too 'Eastern'. Maharaj Ji was changing his look, or, as my dad said, his vibe. Shaking off the whiff of the seventies. No Mansons, Jonestowns, all that, I'd heard my dad say. We can still kiss his feet, but in secret now, because it looks too whacky. Don't mention it at school, okay? Earlier, he'd burned all his copies of the *Divine Times*. Then the meditation pamphlets, satsang programmes and rules for ashram living. All gone. But what I couldn't understand was why our photographs had to go. I liked looking at Dave in a highchair with chocolate on his face or at an old orange cat I didn't remember.

'It feels light to be free of it… stuff, possessions, detritus of life. Doesn't it?' Dad said. 'All possessions are little anchors, keeping you low.'

He hesitated on one photograph, though, and stared at it for a minute. I leaned over to see. It was a snapshot of Dave in a buggy and my Irish nana gripping the handlebars. Me, next to them, eyeing the camera. We were on a hill in Llandudno on a day trip, two summers before. Nana had a train pension and could take us anywhere for £1 each. As always in Wales, it was raining. We shivered in our macs, played on the arcades and had chips for lunch. A happy day.

I watched him. I could see he didn't want to destroy the photograph. I said, 'If you burn that, Dad, is the memory of our day in Llandudno gone?' He turned and looked at me and I thought: can memory be burned out, like the cigarette hole on the back of our sofa? But my memory, while remembering that sofa, doesn't give me what my dad replied.

'Got more in the back if you want to have a look?' The woman pointed to a tray of glass paperweights, so I wandered over to them. Pointless and pretty. It occurred to me that paperweights are for people who aren't going anywhere. You only get a paperweight if you want to be weighed down, whereas paper is about running away: a paper plane, a ticket. I pulled my sunglasses out of my bag; it really was sunny. For the previous few months, intense hallucinatory memories had been coming over me at unexpected moments. Sometimes I could taste my parents' joints in my mouth. Or smell their dusky, sickly patchouli oil. I was in my forties now, Maharaj Ji and that time were decades ago, and yet I often found myself thinking of the old back garden. The next-door dog yapping. Dave kicking a ball about, and the fire in the bin. That particular day. Dad burning photos. Looking past him, I saw Mum in the kitchen with Bill. He was one of the Divine Light Mission Premies. Premies were instructors, named after Prem Rawat, who we knew as Maharaj Ji. Bill was always at ours, picking sesame seeds out of the cracks in his teeth.

I took the paperweight from Dad's photograph box. A blue house was suspended in the glass. I held it in front of my eye and looked through the globe and back to the kitchen window. Bill was leaning close to my mum, touching her hair and whispering. She smiled.

'Dad,' I said to get his attention, but he was smoking, burning, purging, chuckling. He was pretty stoned.

Mum, smiling, said something back to Bill and turned to look out of the window. I'd lowered the paperweight and was staring straight at her; I met her eye. I was nine. I expected her to break her look or turn away, but she didn't. She conveyed to me that she could set everything on fire, even though it was my dad doing the actual burning. It wasn't about Bill, or even my dad. It was something else. She had the power to place a bomb in our house, in our garden or kitchen, and detonate it. She challenged me to stop her. I felt the same destructive impulse myself. She pulled me in and made me complicit. If I am going to destroy everything, her eyes said, then you are part of it too. I sensed danger and shrank back until I was nothing.

Maharaj Ji was a magician who took everything away. My parents worked hard to reach enlightenment, meditating around whatever job they had going at the time. Bill considered himself an anointed saint walking on earth. A representative of a holy spirit. He inhabited our kitchen.

The rent woman and the Provvy woman had different knocks when they came for their money. The rent lady banged on the door fast and angry. The Provvy lady was slow and confident. We hid behind the sofa when they came. These elements – the Guru, Bill's voice in the kitchen, low and much posher than all of us, and our collective anxiety based on the knocking women – were like the weights on Nana's kitchen scales. The weights had to balance perfectly. Otherwise we might tip into my mum's black pit, the open coffins she spoke of when she came to say goodnight.

I leaned back from the tray of paperweights and swung my hand around, but there was nothing there. No clump of hair to ruffle, no sweaty little hand to grab. I had a lurching sense of having lost something vital, a child who had slipped away and disappeared, and I panicked for a second. My son's red hair is easy to spot, and I relaxed when I saw it. My daughter was next to him, shimmering with the inner-moon light she always gave off. My husband was rummaging through a toolbox at the next stand. Car boot professionals, a family of hoarders. Broken families are ten a penny, but they are also the saddest thing, like individual photographs floating around charity shops without an album to live in.

My question was this: if you grow up with a broken family, will you inevitably break yours too? This is what had been agitating me, throwing up these memories, forcing me backwards in time: could I be as destructive as I think my mum felt all those years ago? I had a weird urge to ask this of the SALVAGERS woman, the way we seek advice from strangers.

'You can have the paperweight for a quid,' she said.

'No, I—'

'Actually, have it for free. I don't need it. Trying to get rid of them,' she said, defying the laws of car boot sales. I thought, well, it's a sign. This was my idea: if I could reclaim all the lost and fragile things and reassemble something, a museum, a sense of permanence, an arrangement of items, an exhibition of the lost things, then maybe I could stop everything catching fire. Or stop the anxious feeling I had that the Guru had eaten the central substance of my life. That something fundamental had been stolen from us.

I ran into the kitchen that long-ago day, pushing my way into the space where Bill and my mum were standing near the sink. The room smelled of joints; their smoke ate the walls. One night, my dad, with bright shiny eyes and a twitch in his cheek, stripped the wallpaper in our kitchen. He spent hours drawing a landscape that curled around the sink and the wall near the fridge. Mountains, waterfall, deer, and in the middle a flourish of words saying *Maharaj Ji's Lover*.

Bill looked at me, his body blocking the word *Lover*. I held out the paperweight with the blue house inside that I'd grabbed from the photograph box and turned to Mum. 'Can we keep this one?' I said to her.

We were in deep purge. Getting rid of everything: toys, clothes, wellies, coats, umbrellas, VHS tapes. I had some hiding places, but not many. She took the paperweight from me and held it up in front of her face for a minute. All the light in the world came through it, and that specific blue colour.

Can I see her? Now? Thin, anxious, clever. Attractive and intense when she wanted to be, but skittish and quick to look vulnerable, frail. Moving eyes, difficult to see into her thoughts, always a secret just out of sight. Physically retreating, not touchy-feely. But laughter, too. Funny and quick to get deep into the pulse of whatever psychological jolt was going on in a room. She could walk into a space and suss out the psychodynamics in a second. She knew all the vulnerable points. Young, frustrated, resentful.

'Can I keep this one, Mum?'

Now, as an adult, I am always looking for missing things. I crouch down to examine a scrap of paper on the floor. I glance in skips and bins. Sometimes I snap out of a daydream and panic, as if I've left my laptop on the train. Or my phone in the toilet. Or my child in the car park.

I think this feeling began when my mum took that paperweight out of my hand. With Bill watching and Dad looking the other way, she said, 'It's meaningless, can't you understand that?' and smashed it on the kitchen floor.

I kept a list in my head of all the things I was looking for, but quickly realized it would be too long. I would need to write it all down, all the lost things.

Don't be a materialistic pig, Suzy-Sue. Don't you know it's all just nothing? Nothing.

The things came one after another. All as pointless, beautiful, meaningful, ephemeral, substantial as a paperweight. Cameras, glasses, fur coats, snow globes, hairbrushes, in no order.

I started a notebook called A Catalogue for the Archive of the Museum of My Own Invention. It brought up many questions, such as: Can I be sure the paperweight smashed on the kitchen floor? Because it's harder than you think to break a dense piece of glass like that. So, is my memory trustworthy?

Here, then, the story of a year of salvage. An attempt to remember a life that was disrupted. A method I tried out, examining what was lost or almost forgotten. To find the item or element in real life, or if that wasn't possible, to conjure up its flavour and essence through words and to arrange it in some form of order. To grow up both in a 'cult' and in a working-class world, whatever those words might mean, was a confusing clash of identities or non-identities. I'd never tried to pull the elements apart, let alone arrange them back together into a story. It became important to find a composition for them, to build a house, a museum space and a room. If that wasn't possible, an exhibition at least, with an accompanying catalogue that might or might not be burned one day.

Breton Doll

Where to begin finding the things you've lost?

Estates, houses, utopia, dreams, stuff.

My house is a terrace in an English seaside town on the south coast. The interior is long and thin. The rooms are gloomy, as is often the way with old houses like these. There is mould and a problem with the roof tiles. We've put my daughter's old baby bath under a drip in the attic. Builders tell me the back wall has a 'pig' in it, which is not as bad as subsidence but not great. The backyard is tiny and backs on to a railway embankment. I can't put bird feeders up because rats party with the fat balls.

It's about a mile from the sea, and I can often smell salty seaweed in the air if the weather has been wild. If class is built into the architecture around us, then seaside terraces are shapeshifters. Damp and shabby on a Tuesday afternoon in February, but on a sunny day the bay windows are appealing, almost Mediterranean. It's a far cry from some other houses or rooms I've lived in. And a far cry from Maharaj Ji's ashrams. I was the first in my family to own a home. What a miracle: a house made of history, marriage and words.

The first Christmas in the house, I invited Mum around. I was eight months pregnant. We hadn't spoken to each other for a year until I had announced my pregnancy. With the excitement of the new baby, we both conveniently forgot what our last fight was about and put it aside. Well, I didn't forget, but anyway.

My dad lived in rented accommodation. My mum is in a housing association flat. That Christmas Eve morning, she stepped into the new house and smiled at the tree – a real one, heavily decorated – and stared around, nervous because of our recent estrangement. She walked through the hall, smiling. 'It's nice, it's great, it's nice,' she repeated. 'Just think, you can stay here until you die. If you need to.' I was felled by those words. Stay till you die. An anchoring not possible when you rent. I had an impulse to apologize, but instead asked her if she wanted to do a house-cleansing sage ceremony with me. The roll of dried leaves, the faff of getting it to smoke. Sage is a smell I dislike, but still, I handed the smoking leaves to her. 'Wave it,' I said. 'It gets rid of the bad energy and the past and other people.' I followed her as she walked through the rooms. She wafted smoke and shouted, 'Begone! Begone! Begone!'

Now it was August, tipping into September, and I was going on a quick trip, leaving my family behind. A quick dash before the school mayhem began again.

'Just two nights.' I put water in the dog's bowl, kissed the kids, touched my husband's elbow. The sea fret made the pavement slabs damp. Our house looked sunken in the Anglo-Saxon weather.

I'd seen the Breton doll online.

It was for sale in an antique shop in a small French town. I wanted to get it in person for my Exhibition. I'd started to refer to it as 'Exhibition' in inverted commas in my head. Anyway, it was an excuse to leave home for a brief pocket of time.

The hotel in Dinard was called the Villa Bric à Brac. A sign told me that it was once a marine research station and aquarium owned by a polar explorer. My room was a turret overlooking the harbour. My phone buzzed before I'd even put my bag down. It was my brother, Dave, texting: *Mum's bad again. Give me a call.* I opened a window and looked out at the harbour. Flagpoles clanged, seagulls scrapped in the air. The hotel was so nautical it felt as though I was on a boat. With phones, we may as well not travel. We're digital hostages; they make everywhere the same. I turned it off and threw it on the bed. *Mum's bad again.* We had agreed a protocol after the previous crisis. First, talk on the phone, remind her of the Recovery Centre number, but if it escalates one or both of us go round to keep an eye on her. There was a tidal, endless rhythm to it.

On one of Mum's 'bad times', I had met Dave as arranged in the pub on the corner of her road before we went knocking on her door. We had a coffee. Dave's eyes were ringed with black shadows. His babies were still at the up-all-night stage. I had a pathetic bag of gifts for Mum. Prawn sandwich, Nescafé. A fridge magnet. Items that might seem insignificant but which I hoped might operate like tiny floats, holding her up. I had such a desire to be a saviour. I believed I could take the weight from Dave too, whose appearance made me feel guilty for some reason. Dave stared like a zombie into the froth of his cappuccino. I ran my hand over the dragonfly fabric of the chair. We said nothing. She'd spent the previous evening blasting us with texts about how terrible we were. She specialized in verbal arrows, fire-outs of anguish and despair. Her messages switched from vicious barbs to suicidal threats. We never, ever, knew if she was going to do it. We lived constantly with the threat. We couldn't even stay angry with her, because we knew it was real. Her pain was always worse than ours.

We knocked that day. She took a long time to answer, and when she did, she held a cushion against herself as if stemming a wound. She looked pale, older than usual.

'Mum, why did you do it?' We stepped inside. Her flat is one room, with a tiny kitchenette. The bed and the sofa are next to each other, and the only other area she has is a small bathroom. Dolls are arranged in all available spaces. Small, large, plastic and knitted. All colours.

She pointed to the window. 'They are taking down the window boxes.' She had no garden but tended magnificent window boxes that overflowed with blousy geraniums and trails of ivy.

Dave lurked by the door. I could tell he desperately wanted to get out of there. I sat on the bed.

'It's so unfair,' Mum said.

'Why are they taking them down?'

'People have complained about the pigeons, but that's her upstairs, not me. She feeds them.'

'I'm sorry,' I said.

'I haven't been able to sleep for a few nights,' she said, wiping her watery eyes. 'I was dreaming of Birch Avenue.' This was the council house she'd grown up in on the edge of Crewe.

'Maybe drink less coffee if you can't sleep?'

She sniffed. 'I just keep dreaming about it and waking and then... self-medicating. I don't know why.'

Self-medicating was a new expression she'd learned either from the Recovery Centre or online. She stared at the floor, desolate. It was always like this, me trying to reach her. She said terrible things in the night, and in the blank daylight it was impossible either to accuse or to understand.

'I remember that doll,' I said, picking up a floppy rag doll that was decades old.

'I don't know how it's lasted,' she said. A pained smile. 'I had others, but they're gone.' Dave and I got out of there as quickly as we could. We felt guilty for doing so but were unwilling to be drawn down into the sadness. That was how it went, on repeat, ad infinitum; we were officially the world's worst children.

A note on the door of the antique shop in Dinard said *Vient de sortir sera bientôt de retour*. I could make out wardrobes, rocking horses and teacups, but no sign of an owner. I went back to the hotel bar for an early supper of seaweed-infused bread and kept phoning the shop, but no answer. I peered out of the circular port windows. My kids would like it here, I thought. The round windows, the seaweed bread. Family: Me. Husband. Two kids. Dog.

'How did we produce such a square?' my dad used to say when I insisted on going in via the entry door and exiting through the exit door. Clipboard Sue. Checking on the rules. Organizing Annie. 'What do you want to go to university for?' they'd say, as I stomped past the meditators with my books and homework. 'Go to Paris! Go to Berlin! Or take a trip! That will get you further.'

Nobody answered the phone in the antique shop all afternoon. I was starting to get cross. Mainly because I felt like an idiot. I could have ordered the doll online, but no, I'd made it a whole thing. I sat in my turret room and wondered if my husband would remember to plait my daughter's hair before she got into bed so it wouldn't get into too much of a tangle. I thought of her most recent school photograph and how I needed to put in an order before it was too late.

Once, there were childhood photographs hanging around from my early years, despite the instructions, the *agyas* and the Guru's demands. I remembered one of my parents' shot-gun wedding day in April 1973. Mum, aged nineteen, in a miniskirt, long boots and a turtleneck. She holds a strappy purse with both hands over me, hidden inside her belly. Dad, standing next to her, rocking a full-on seventies-cool look. Later that week, they were thrown out of their flat due to my mum's condition and crept back to their parents with a begging bowl. Mum didn't know what a bidet was. Nor a placenta. When clots of blood blobbed into the white enamel bowl, she used a paper towel to scoop out the gunk and dropped it into a metal bin. Nana was so furious with her for running away and then sloping home that she refused to come to the birth. Males, even hippy ones, stayed away from labour wards in those days. This photograph was long-lost now.

She knitted so much she kept running out of wool. Socks and cardigans to keep my premature, yellow, shrivelled and unlikely-to-survive body warm in the incubator. Mum was allowed to come in and look at me through a glass window once a day. She always kept a doll with her. A Breton doll with a yellowing cellophane face and a strange white tubular hat. She had decided it was a good luck charm that would keep me alive.

Three separate times she was sent home without me. She sat on her bed, rolling a cigarette, grappling with the tangible absence I had now become. Jaundice. Premature. Unwanted. Wanted/Unwanted. I was released from the hospital eventually. 'Don't smoke around this baby,' the nurses said. 'Her lungs are premature and bad.'

I stared at the harbour's edge and tried to ignore the siren call from Mum. I felt it intensely, telepathically. I think it came from knitting. A clamouring clatter. Her knitting was wild, without a pattern, but eerily accurate. Grey seagulls or odd-eyed mermaids. Sometimes I woke in the night, convinced I could hear the tap of her needles. Sitting on the balcony of the turret, I gave up all resistance and called her. She answered straight away. I tried to identify her state of mind from the sound of her voice or her breathing.

'Yes?'

'Hi. Did you get the results?' Last year she'd had pneumo-
nia and couldn't shake it. She was exhausted after years of
turning patients over in bed. Cleaning bedsores, changing
catheters, wiping shit and checking blood. She had been sent
for extra tests and they had come back with COPD: chronic
obstructive pulmonary disease. Incurable. Life expectancy
depended on how far gone it was.

'What do you mean?'

'I mean, did they tell you the exact stage of the lung
disease?'

'Oh, they don't talk about stages,' she said. I looked
out at the Brittany sea, the shifting greys and the bright
light. Over on the island on the opposite side of the bay
was an enormous Mary, casting her good wishes to the
sailors. I tried to interpret information from the sound of
her voice.

'Dave says you've been phoning him. Getting upset?'

'Yes.' Then she started talking fast, about people I didn't
know. A friend of hers from the hospital had been looking
after a man with green gums who'd only eaten leaves for a
month. A cousin. A neighbour.

Mum kept talking. I waited for a pause in her usual chatter as I looked at the sky. It was going to rain any minute.
Brittany had the same weather as Llandudno. Ireland. South
coast of England.

'Are you listening to me?' she said, and I wished I could
take hold of her knitting and hold it aloft, as if she were the
champion of the world's knitting competition and I was
something in the team – the coach or funder or long-time

supporter – and together we would celebrate it and say, 'That's great!'

'Yes,' I said. There was a quiet second before they came. I'd heard these words many times before, as a child, teenager, adult. I knew the lull. The wheezy breath followed by litany. *What's the point? Can't stand it. Nowhere to go. Nobody cares.* Every word is huge, heavy. A trapped loop. *Are you listening to me?* I don't know. Perhaps it wasn't the right moment, but I said it anyway, to stop the words. 'Mum. Do you remember the tapes, Mum, playing all the time?'

'What?'

'Maharaj Ji tapes.'

The cough-cough-coughing. Her words faltered. I listened to the struggling breath.

'You okay?'

'Yes, tight chest today. Steroids. What did you say?' Selective hearing. Wind in the trees, howling in the head. The seagulls getting louder and louder. I felt the creak of a trapdoor and the past opening between us.

She projected an enormous amount of meaning on to these dolls, or so it seemed to me, a person who never played with or understood them. Mum was being coerced into throwing her childhood Breton doll away. Not flames this time, but a vast heap of rubbish in the back of Bill's car, ready to be dumped.

'I don't know. I've had it forever.' She was cradling the Breton doll and frowning. I was young, I don't know how old exactly, but I was interested. She so often purged my stuff, and now it was her turn. Bill leaning next to her.

Dad rocking forwards. One of them said, 'It's made of bits of wood and stuffing and nothing else. It is nothing else. Let it go.'

With an Irish dad who liked the bottle and the races and a barmaid mum who hid the rent money from him, Mum hadn't had many toys when small. Her Crewe was the sixties, whereas mine was the eighties. In some ways different but in others the same. Wet roofs. Twisted railings. Rude graffiti on the walls of the concrete underpass. The washing in the garden getting caught in the rain. The part of me that had been interested now shifted into outrage on her behalf.

'Don't do it,' I said. 'I don't think you should throw away the doll.' I was the kind of kid who was always there, watching everything, underfoot.

Bill, or possibly Dad, said, 'You look beautiful today, Lynda. Think of him. Think of how it feels. More important. Guruji love. Feel it.' One of them kissed her forehead and stepped back. I knew what that doll meant to her, because she raged if I touched it.

'I think those tapes did something to our heads, our brains,' I said. 'Do you?'

She said nothing.

'Mum, do you remember Bill? I keep thinking about him.' I followed a seagull's journey above the bay as I listened for her answer, but she was gone. She'd hung up in a fit of coughing. When I tried again her phone was turned off.

There was an email: *Vous pouvez récuperer votre poupée maintenant.*

I WhatsApped home and spoke to my daughter. 'What's it like?' she said, and I felt bad about leaving her behind with school and nothingy days.

'Not that special.' I didn't tell her the hotel was like a boat.

'Liar.' We both giggled. She showed me her new glasses. 'I look like you. I'm going to write like you and be like you. I'll go to hotels and look for things.'

'Great,' I said. 'That's great.' I loved her so much. I was full of the feeling of it, the bright shine of it. She told me about her homework. I didn't quite listen. Instead, I looked at her eyes, at the shape of her brows. She didn't speak at school. There were tests, and an educational psychologist had been brought in and Mum had said, 'I was like that. But no one tested me.'

The Breton doll was expensive and fragile. I didn't know if it was the right one or even if it was from the right era. It had a wide skirt hemmed with lace and a yellowing face with the eyes rubbed out. She will invent her own knitting patterns for it, I thought. I packed a French newspaper around it to carry it home. As I did, I kept thinking: who's to blame? And: how to save?

Railway Terrace,
Late 1970s

The day has never started. It was grey and dark in the morning, and at lunchtime, then darker still by four o'clock. Dad begins with a dot in the middle of the page and sketches around it, moving the pencil in circles. He shades soft lines until the Guru's face appears. He's copying from a photograph in the *Divine Times*.

I'm drawing too. I draw houses, join the triangle roof with the square to make a solid house. Doors. Corridors. Kitchens. I like squares and corners. I like circles. I like the compass and the protractor and the ruler. Dad is wearing his green army surplus jumper, and now and then I touch the felt elbow pads. 'Do you like my house?' I say. Chimney, window frame, tree in the garden. Fence.

'Sure,' he says, 'but why don't you have a go at Maharaj Ji? It will help you to understand.'

I tune in to the sound of the cassette.

Come to the shelter of Guru's grace, Come with your heart and your soul. Cross the worldly ocean with your devotion. And attain the supreme goal. Jai Dev, Jai Satgurudev...

I look at his sketch. Smiling face, an Indian crown and lots of jewels. I can't imagine how to do it. I shake my head. Dad puts his hand on mine. 'Try,' he says. He is smoking, smiling, eyes shiny. 'Draw with love, from the heart.'

'What do you mean?'

'Draw so that it feels… intimate.'

I look at the Guru's face on my dad's page and back at the house on mine. Next to my house, I have a go at Guru Maharaj Ji's head. I try a circle and a crown, but it doesn't look right.

'Draw him like he's your special friend. That way you can talk to him in your mind. You can call him Master. With each stroke of the pencil, you start to know you love him. Feel it? You know you are ready. Nothing else makes sense, everything else is dust. You can do that through drawing, you know, right?'

I look round to see where Mum is, but she's out. I try swirls, an eye, a mouth, but it all just looks like lines.

'You've got to go deeper,' he says, blowing smoke into my hair. 'Into the page. Fill in the pieces. You'll see, he's already there. You've got everything inside you that you need to see him. He's waiting for you. Can you see it?'

There's a noise in the other room. Dad goes to see if it's Dave or the dog. I run to the bathroom to get away from the drawing for a minute and pick at the cracked, dry soap that none of us use. I scrape at the black circle of stuff – what is it? A sort of mould that's in between the bathroom tiles.

I can't put it off any longer, so I go back and stare at my page. I fiddle, I pull off one of my socks, even though it's cold and the fire hasn't been lit yet. I stare at the paper, but I can't see it.

He comes back and stands behind me and peers over at my drawings. 'Don't put your faith in houses, Suzy-Sue. The wolf comes, they blow away, the floods carry them off. They are made of nothing but paper, and what's the good of that?'

That night I listen to them shouting. It's always money. Paying this. Paying for that. When I'm big, I think, burrowing deeper into my bed, I won't worry about wolves taking my house away. I'll make sure my house is real.

Oh, Guruji. You are all-powerful.

There is nothing in this world that you cannot do. Please guide me. And protect me. Forever and ever. Bhole Shri Satgurudev Maharaj Ki Ja.

It plays all afternoon. Our front door opens from the living room directly on to the street. Another noise: Ker-chunn-ker-chunnn. The ker-chunn-ker-chunnn comes from the Bombardier site. It's called the Melts. Part of Crewe Works, at the bottom of our yard. A huge factory, where Dad says they make trains, take them apart, repair them or destroy them. At the end of the day, a horn blows. The streets fill with bicycles and men in blue boiler suits with metal clips around their ankles.

Inside our house, it's different. We have no indoor bath, no indoor loo, no garden. Shadows float through the yellow-lit kitchen. The tea comes in boxes with swirly writing on the side. Pans simmer on the gas ring, frothing grey lentil juice.

Jars are full of dried beans that look like eyes: lentils, butter beans, borlotti. Dal for breakfast, lunch, tea. People over for satsangs; strangers wrap themselves in one of my mum's knitted blankets. They stay for a week then go to India or Afghanistan. How far is India from Crewe?

Satsang nights: all round to meditate, so early to bed. My mum presses PLAY on the cassette player. Dave in the cot, me in bed, with my pencil. I draw lines on the wall. Swirls. Go for it, drawing, drawing. Then, when it's time, I lie on the floor. A place where I can pull the carpet back. Put my head on the floorboards, press my ear down and listen to the words creeping up through the cracks.

'And I used to drive him around, you know. When he did the second UK tour.' That's Bill speaking. 'Magic days.'

Dad's voice rising. 'Yeah, something is missing in my life. It's like there's something I must get to, but I can't. There's something I need, but I don't know what it is. There's something that's supposed to be there. That need for love.'

(Where is Mum? I don't know.)

Bill, shouting at Dad: 'What would you do for him, John?'

A woman shouting, not my mum. Angry? I squish my ears harder against the floor.

'What would you give up?'

My dad: 'Money. Self. Life. Home. Everything.'

'Are you devoted enough?' Another man's voice.

'I think so.'

'Are you proving it enough? Are you showing it on every level of your life?'

'I think so.'

'Would you give up this life, this home, this family? Would you give up Lynda? Would you give up your kids?' Mumbling sound.

Bill: 'The satsanging is hard, I know. Have some water. Breathe.'

Dad, muffled. Cough. Laughter.

Bill again: 'Would you do anything for him?'

Dad: 'Yes.'

Bill: 'Anything?'

'Yes.'

A woman: 'Would you give up your kids, your life?'

'Yes.'

Someone else: 'This is when we will know you are ready. Do you think you are ready?'

'Yes.'

Bill: 'I'm not sure. I'm not sure yet, John. I'm just not sure.'

I stand up. I open the door and draw a line from the handle, all along the landing wall. I move to the staircase and keep going, a wobbly grey pencil line down the wall of the stairs. The door opens. It's Dad, sweating, hair sticking up from his head, eyes red. 'Sue, what are you doing up?'

I close my eyes. Pretend I'm sleepwalking. Hold the pencil tight.

'Sue?' Hand on my shoulder, shaking me. I open my eyes.

'Drawing,' I say. I put the pencil between my teeth.

'Sleep. Get to sleep.' I am shoved up the stairs, hustled back into the room. I lie in bed, but the smoke is invasive, coming through floorboard cracks, circling. I look up at a Y-shaped crack on the ceiling and it makes me think of a tree: trunk, branches, ladders, climb out. Breathe, but it's no good, I'm coughing.

Mum comes in with Vicks and lights the candle in the oil burner. She puts her hand on my chest for a minute and I wait.

'Sue, you have to stop coughing so we can finish meditating.'

'Will you stay?'

A frown, hair tucked behind the ear, turning face. She is retreating, closing the door. I make a triangle of myself in the bed, focus on the Y-shaped crack and push a pillow into my mouth, far enough to make my eyes water.

'Did you know, Sue,' says Bill, 'that when people leave the Divine Light Mission they shatter into a million pieces?'

He is a wizard with brick dust under his fingernails. He cracks walnut shells by smashing jam jars on them. I am on the kitchen step, examining coal. Good coal, bad coal, depending on shininess. If you cover your face and hair with coal dust, there will be trouble. His leg is giant, like a tree trunk. He blocks out the sun with his cowboy hat with corks dangling off the rim. How old am I? About five, I think. How old is he? One hundred.

'Did you know, Sue,' Bill says, filling up the door frame, 'that if a person tells anyone the Divine Secrets without authorization, that person turns into cockroaches?'

I wriggle away from him and go into the kitchen, lean against the gas meter slot to escape scattering cockroaches. I'm unhappy about the focus on a brother. Clackety-clack,

Mum's knitting needles, a cardigan for me, socks for the new baby. I hate lentils.

Meditate. Meditate. Mediate. Reach for the Light and become the Sun. Become One. I ask my dad to teach me. 'No,' he says. 'It's for grown-ups. You're too little.'

But I beg. I want to do what they are all doing. I lean against his arm, squeeze it until he can't ignore me.

'Okay.' A long line of smoke into my face, a sleepy smile. 'Close your eyes. Blow a bubble in your lungs,' he says. I do it. 'Now count to twenty, can you do that? One two three four, through the left nostril and out of the right... any thoughts that come, let them float in a balloon away from your head.'

It gives me lights behind my eyes and the beginning of a headache, but I don't tell him.

'Let go of your mind, little Sue,' he says, 'and just be. Your thoughts aren't real, they are bubbles, they are nothing.'

I peep out through my eyelids. If my thoughts are a bubble, then when it floats away, am I dead?

Later, I go to the kitchen to ask him: will I die if I let my thoughts go? Am I still me if my brain is turned off? But now Dad is sitting with his forehead on the table. The dog stares at the food bowl, nothing in it. Bill stands behind Dad, saying, 'You must feel it, not know it, feel it, you must feel it, only then are you ready, only then, only then.' They turn to look at me, the two men, and it is Bill who shouts. 'Get out. Get out. Get out.' My dad's face is twisted, ugly and crying.

Bill fills the house, takes up all the corners of it. The others are shadowy, coming and going, but he stays. I don't know when he will go.

I can't find my mum. She's slipping through door frames as if going out, carrying the baby, who cries. Now he's got colic, now he's got chickenpox in his mouth. She has a row of dolls on a shelf in her room, but I can't touch them. I can't catch anyone's hands. Shiny eyes; it is always smoky. They are working to get the Knowledge, or they are changing the nappies. Children aren't allowed to follow. I'm not sure where they are all going.

During the war, the walls and roofs of Crewe Works were painted with fake houses to trick the Germans. We walk this road every day on the way to Nana's, alongside the Melts. I can't see inside, but I imagine massive fire pits and claw grippers, coming down in great pointed snatches. Like the machine on Rhyl pier, grabbing at teddies but rigged to miss. Trains coming apart. The parts melting and crushers crushing. If I time my in-breath with my right leg as we walk home from the shops in the rain, me holding on to Dave's buggy, then I can step out of this life and slip through the walls of the trick houses to get away from what Nana calls the Luftwaffe. It is a good hiding place, inside the grit stuff that sticks the bricks together. I feel, privately, that the fake, painted houses are real. And the real ones are not where I am supposed to be.

Typewriter

There is something special about being in a provincial museum. The gloomy corridors and glass cases. The smell of oak, varnish and detergent. The dimmed lights and the sense that the past is touchable through the gathered artefacts. Everyday items, now on a pedestal, become history.

I trailed my mum and daughter around the narrow corridors. I had been visiting this museum regularly for a few weeks to 'capture' the stories of older workshop participants. As if memories could be netted like chaffinches and trapped. I had brought Mum and my daughter along for a day out. I wanted to tell them my idea. 'Exhibition,' I said. 'Or, museum of myself... Or, of ourselves...'

Mum moved slowly, trying to hide her coughing. I wanted to comfort her in some way, but it was difficult to know how to begin. Along the line words had stopped working for us, but underneath the spiky silences I always wished I could offer her peace. Especially peace within her tangled-sounding lungs.

My daughter drifted ahead to the other room, which was called 'the Library' although there were no books. Mum and I stood together next to a cabinet and looked down at a Smith

Corona typewriter from the twenties. According to the label, the typewriter in front us of had once belonged to a woman called Vera Pragnell. She had set up a commune on a heath near the village. 'A utopian dream,' I said, reading out the information. 'Vera Pragnell had a vision.'

I read more. It was called 'the Sanctuary.' She was an heiress from the north whose father had owned an enormous textile company. She bought land and advertised in the newsletter of the Fellowship of Reconciliation (a pacifist, interfaith organization) that she was giving away land for free to anyone who needed it. She offered food, cash and shelter to needy travellers. Unsurprisingly, soon the place was invaded by all sorts. Anarchists, communists, travellers, actors.

'I would have come,' Mum said, sighing. 'I would have joined in with her dream.' I didn't doubt it.

'I've got to go and do the workshop older now. Are you both going to stay here?'

'We'll go and look in the village and then come back,' Mum said, smiling.

I looked down at the typewriter keys, the arms and the roller. The times when we didn't, or couldn't, speak to one another were like wormholes in time. Days, weeks, in some cases years, passed; life happened. The rifts came out of rage, followed by exhaustion. I compulsively wrote to her during disconnected periods. I didn't want to, but the force of words kept coming and needed to be deposited and contained somewhere. Diaries, notebooks, unsent letters. Right back to the Christmas I'd got a typewriter. After that, word processors and primitive laptops. Later, phones. The various devices, pages and hard drives are all lost now. Now it was texting or messaging, but never emailing. I could never get it right, the thing I was trying to say.

Mum wobbled slightly, as if the floor was not to be trusted. I held her elbow, but she shrugged away from me.

I read a little more about Vera Pragnell. 'Look, Mum,' I said, 'she was a follower of Flemish mystic John van Ruysbroeck's system called "the Ladder of Spiritual Love". It involved purging, getting rid of superfluous things and following "the Way".'

'Sounds all right to me,' she said. I couldn't tell if she was being wry or serious.

I continued reading out. 'But things went wrong. She married Dennis Earle, a friend of Aleister Crowley, and fights about the land and money began.'

Mum was drifting away, looking for my daughter.

'Similar to Maharaj Ji, a bit, Mum, don't you think?'

I glanced over. My mentioning the Guru and other old ghosts was a new thing. Recently I'd had this strong compulsion to grab things and haul them from the corridors of the past and shove them into a brightly lit car park. But Mum was moving off, pretending not to hear. She started to cough, the deep bronchitis sound, the shudders. She knocked into the door frame, swore, and moved on. She was always at war with the places she was in, it seemed. I watched her join my daughter and the two of them pick through things on a table set up in the corner selling books and cakes.

And then a segment of her – by which I mean our – life came to me.

It was Brighton. Years ago. She had left my dad and was living in a basement flat. The window was at pavement level. I was living in London and was in my late twenties.

She phoned late one afternoon. 'A man masturbates outside my window. The police don't care, the landlord doesn't care.'

'What?'

'I have to have the curtains closed all the time. I am living in a hole.' I couldn't tell if there was a slurred edge to her voice or not.

Grabbing my bag, I made excuses into the fluorescently lit office. I struggled through the dead-faced commuters at Victoria and squished on the train down to Brighton. I walked fast from the station to her flat, a basement bedsit in a Georgian terrace on the seafront. I banged on her door. She didn't open it for ages, and when she did, she didn't seem drunk. More as if she were in the aftermath of something. A difficult night, a problematic few days, I guessed.

I stood in her doorway. 'What's going on,' I asked, 'with this man at your window?' She waved her hand, dismissive and a bit sheepish. I went into the small room and was overwhelmed with the stuff arranged on the walls. Pictures. Cut-outs from newspapers. Photos. She had covered every single part of her bedsit with a colourful thing. Little toys and cushions everywhere. It was the opposite of purged; it was suffocatingly material.

'I read the thing you published about the woman and her daughters,' she said, putting the kettle on.

It was one of the first things I'd put out into the world as a writer, a published piece of creative non-fiction about letters I'd found in a box. It contained letters to a mother from her daughters. The return letters from the mother were missing, and I'd tried to fill in the gaps. I sat on the edge of her bed with a low feeling coming in my stomach. Precognition. Familiar paths. I'd come from London for reasons other than the man standing at the window, who possibly didn't even exist.

'Ah, okay,' I said. 'Did you like it?'

'Yeah, it was great... but...' Her hands were shaking, I noticed, as she poured milk into the cups.

'What?' There was a long pause.

'I thought it was ironic, you know, you writing about a mother and a daughter, and I thought it was typical... obvious, you know... that you would blame the mother.'

I took a deep breath. I'd been tricked. I was trapped. I squeezed my hand to figure out what to say.

'Why are you here?' she said, turning on me, her eyes a little wilder now. 'You should be in fancy London. In fancy Paris. In Syria or one of those war places you go to that I can't think about.'

'You called me, Mum. A couple of hours ago. About the man at your window.'

She looked surprised at this, and I stamped down anger. I come in peace, I told myself. An orange trumpet of fungus blossomed above her window frame. I put my fingertips on my eyelids and pushed on them for a second.

'I can't live here any more,' she said in a quiet voice.

I moved from her bed and perched on the edge of a small sofa. I focused on the row of snow globes along her windowsill. I tuned in to what she was telling me. Seventy per cent of her wages from her nursing assistant job at the hospital went on rent for this dingy shitty mouldy flat. She flapped paperwork near my face. She was writing at least once a week to the council. Fighting for a housing associating flat. I blew air out of my mouth. This was why I had been summoned; this was what she needed to tell me.

'Every week, Mum? It's a waste of energy, they will just bin them.'

She has to join an online system to bid for a housing association flat. That's the system. That's what you have to do to be housed as a nurse around here.

'I don't do computers,' she said. She was raging. 'I keep telling them. I have no computer. I can't do that.'

'Shall I do it for you?'

'Dave's been doing it.'

She moved around the bedsit in a state of intense agitation. I was sucked downwards and felt helpless, full of revulsion. I'd come from the mess of my own life. A chaotic houseshare, entry-level administrative office work, slogging the extra hours required to clamber up the slippery pole of success. But it was nothing compared to this bedsit in Brighton. Another universe. There was no correlation; I was ashamed of myself for trying to escape this. Writing stories and endlessly starting a novel on the edges of the working day.

A car alarm went off in the street. God, I wanted to run. Bad daughter.

'I keep writing to them. I can't do the computer bidding system. I have to do it by paper.' Her phone rang then, and she screamed out.

'Bloody hell, Mum,' I said, 'what's up? You're so twitchy.' She threw her phone across the room and it clattered down near the door of her fridge. I went over and picked it up.

'All day they call me. They never stop. Like, ten times a day. Night-time even, like now.'

'Who?'

'Look at my phone,' she said. 'See, seven times today.' I looked up the number on my phone. It was a debt collectors' chase. It probably dated back to the Burton's catalogue from the 1980s. School shoes for us bought on the never-never. I remembered her smoking cigarettes and flicking through them at the kitchen table. It only occurs to me now that hire purchase catalogues were the opposite of Maharaj Ji's teachings.

'I'll see if I can help,' I said, backing towards the door. It was like being under a glass dome with a panicking bird. Or being sucked into a nightmare. She gave me a defiant look.

'I might as well go to the sea and die. I have nothing. I am nothing. You don't care. You just live your life in London…'

Something cracked in the side of my head, a fissure. I knew I should be sympathetic, but instead I was pulling away. Part of me wanted to reach out – Mum, please, you are safe, it's okay. The other part wanted to escape the clay turrets and potholes of our sticky past. I picked up my bag and walked out. I thought: if I don't go now, I might lose it. What that meant, I didn't know.

I walked to the end of her road and crossed over the promenade. It was pouring with rain. I hesitated, put my hand on the railings and looked out at the black sodden nothing that was the sea at night. I figured if she were going to do it, then she would. I couldn't stop anything. As I walked, I looked at the glowing, warm rooms of the flats on the seafront. High ceilings and sash windows. Brighton hadn't fully turned yet. It was not quite gentrified. The side streets still whiffed of despair, especially during the off-season.

Finally, my frustration tipped into sadness: I'm sorry, I'm sorry. I'm sorry about the cost of the shoes and the debt collectors still chasing after all these years.

I'd missed the last train back to London by four minutes. It was almost one in the morning. I sat on a bench near the closed coffee kiosk and watched a couple of pigeons attempt to peck each other's eyes out. I would wait until the first commuter train set off at 5.45. Two men were holding each other by the elbows, talking intensely. Impossible to know if it was romantic or violent, or both.

Not to have enough money to pay your rent, even though you work hard cleaning bedsores and changing catheters, gives life a particular flavour. It's low-gnawing tedium. A stomach ache that starts small and spreads around the body. It's a free-fall panic feeling that increases as anxiety builds. It accelerates age, creasing the brow and eyes and crevicing the skin. It contracts eyes and lungs. It carves space in the body for disease and strain. It decreases immunity, it exposes weaknesses. It hurts. It's real pain. It's boring, it's unstoppable. I'm sorry. I'm sorry. I'm sorry, I thought. But I couldn't go back.

'I'd like to live in that Vera Pragnell's Sanctuary,' Mum said, holding my daughter's hand. 'I can imagine myself really fitting in there.'

Writing was difficult for some of the participants of the workshop, so I recorded their stories. The museum was entirely run by volunteers. All women, all over seventy-five.

'Do I speak into it?' Betty shouted. The autumn wind rattled at the windows of the museum, adding to the sonic feedback.

'Just talk normally,' I said. 'The microphones will pick you up.'

The ladies were buttoned-up and nicely turned out in pastel cashmere, lipstick and pearl earrings. They held their handbags on their knees. The youngest was ninety-two, the eldest ninety-eight.

Their eyes watered, and their thin, frail voices were from another era. The carers who pushed their wheelchairs were offensively fleshy and shinily young in contrast.

'Are we ready, everyone?' My big idea was to talk about wedding dresses. I imagined them sharing memories of silks and ruffles. I thought they would share the great narrative of their lives. But it turned out that the dresses were sold or lost decades ago. They spoke of husbands as if fondly remembering a distant cousin. Children were faint ghosts.

'Where do you live, dear?' Betty asked.

'Not far,' I said. 'Worthing, just over the hill.'

She turned to me. 'Do you have a family?'

'Yes, husband, two children.' Nods, smile; it was as it should be. Brenda showed me a photograph of herself as a Wren, standing next to her husband. 'He's very handsome,' I said.

'Do you think so?' She looked doubtful. 'Take it.' She poked the small, framed photograph in my direction. 'Have it.'

'Oh, my goodness, no,' I said. It was the same with all of them. They had been asked to bring mementoes and were affronted when I wouldn't take their offerings. Medals. Jewellery. Extremely precious photographs.

'My house is gone now. I don't know where the box is with my photographs... my flat is gone...' they said. Or versions of it. 'My daughter-in-law had it. My cousin's son took it. I don't know where it all is now. All the things from the house. I'm not sure if the house sold or not. Take it, will you have it? Please?'

'No, Brenda, I can't.' I glanced over at the carers, who were all chatting and facing the other way. If I could, I would take their things and cherish them for them. I wanted to take them and look after them. But I couldn't; it was unethical. I felt enough of a thief stealing their stories.

Afterwards, I found my mum and daughter in the attached community centre. There was a large bay window facing the street and in it a sign saying *Pop-Up Museum of the Self*. 'What's that?' my daughter asked.

The manager, a wispy woman in her seventies, said, 'That is the idea of one of Margaret's granddaughters, it's a... what does she call it, Mary? Oh, a person can create a museum of themselves to share. It is revolving. The things stay for a day or so, or longer, a week.'

We looked at the items on display: a doll's house, a sewing box, embroidery frames with stitches, a row of miniature cups and saucers. We put our names down to have a Museum of the Self slot. We thanked the ladies and stood in the doorway, looking out at the rain.

'Shall I run and get the car, Mum, so you don't get wet?'

I left them there and wandered through the village towards my car. This is it, I thought. I will make it better. Sort it out and stop the pain. I had faith in the arrangement of lost things. Why? Was it reclamation? I was sometimes overcome with appetite and greed when driving around pretty Sussex villages. It was as if I wanted to eat the roofs and bricks. I had lusty covetousness for ownership of land, brick and place, and the feeling of it came into my drawings and my writings. I desired a house like those in the childhood books I had loved. One that survives wars and is imbibed with history and secret gardens. I thought of my Irish nana, whose family were servants working for the 'Big House'. All the houses in my family were temporary. Bedsits, lodgings. Boarding houses. Rented rooms, council houses. Always insecure, houses that can disappear. If you live in places that don't belong to you, then how do you find space to tell your story? I didn't know how to explain to Mum that I'd been collecting things and thinking about an exhibition of our lost stuff.

My daughter sang from the back seat as I drove the twenty minutes through the Downs to Worthing. Mum turned and smiled, touching my daughter's hair. 'Imagine if the teachers saw you now,' she said, looking down at her. 'They wouldn't think you so quiet, they would hear your voice.'

That evening my phone pinged, and despite our nice day the messages started again.

I've wasted my life.

I don't want to do this any more.

Thick and fast, like dripping poison. Despite the singing in the car, despite the warm, cosy sound of rain on the museum roof.

I immediately got a headache. I thought: there must be another way for us.

I'd asked a specialist I'd spoken to a few months before if cults were to blame.

'To blame for what?' The woman with rimless glasses had a slight northern tinge to her voice and had dedicated her life to helping 'cult victims'.

'The state my parents are in. We are all in. Being left spinning with nothing, but we can't get rid of these echoes in our head.'

The specialist looked at me. With her glasses, my glasses and the two Zoom screens, there was a lot of glass between us.

'I tried emailing Prem Rawat,' I said. 'Guru Maharaj Ji.'

'Oh yes? What do you hope to get from him?'

'I find it difficult that the Divine Light Mission is written out of history. That he and his current organization won't admit it existed. That all the people of that time were left with nothing. It's like a collective hallucination or something. That they ended up with no money. Nothing. Many of them gave the organization their houses. Decades of their lives. Any savings.'

'No response?'

'I've had nothing. The headquarters are in Malibu. But no one in his organization answers my emails, though they do pop up to argue with ex-members on the forums.'

'Hmm, yes. Have you spoken to your parents about it directly?'

'No. A bit with my dad. A teeny bit with my mum.'

'What do you think will happen when you talk to them? To her?'

'I think I will make them regret their entire lives and feel terrible about them. I don't want to do that. They already seem to be feeling bad enough about themselves, and at any moment my mum might… and it would be… she is always, always on the edge of them…'

'You think you have that much power over them?'

'Maybe.' I told the specialist that sometimes I'm haunted by memories of these figures from the past, Bill and others. How I can't get the feeling of being sealed up. It's as if whatever was the boundary or border of myself – my private entity – was invaded at some point, and I can't find that missing thing. I am convinced I remain open to invasion. I can never find something I am looking for.

'Blaming others won't help you,' the specialist said. 'It means you are still out of control. You need to reframe. You need to be responsible for yourself.'

Tinkling crystal words came into my head. I couldn't sleep, so I moved around the house like an automaton, sort of tidying up but not really. The house smelled of the chips I'd cooked earlier. There was a draught coming up through the floorboards. The gutter was obviously blocked again, because the rain was coming along the windowpane. It would be seeping into our walls. I was agitated, and as I knew they would, the words in my head got stronger: 'We know a secret and you are not allowed to know it.' Scraping fingernails in the dust of the bricks. Flinging tiles from the roof.

The voice had gone Irish, I don't know why: 'We own your mammy. She's ours. She's ours and she always will be you feck feck feck feck. And you'll never get her back and don't try.'

When I looked at my phone, I saw my own face reflected back, fragmenting. Underneath was Maharaj Ji's face, just as it had looked in our kitchen shrine all those years ago, laughing at me.

Council House, 1980

'Did you hear the news about your dad, Sue? Starting "on the railways", what a good little citizen.' Bill punches Dad in the arm, playful-not-playful. Dad winces.

We've moved from the Melts to an estate on the other side of Crewe. An indoor toilet, three bedrooms, coal shed, normal shed and a garden. Maharaj's cassettes are kept on the bookcase in the living room with titles written on the side. PMT 50 FRANKFURT GERMANY 11/28/76, PMT 51 ATLANTIC CITY, NEW JERSEY 12/17/76, PMT 53 PORTLAND, OREGON 1/30/77. PUJA FESTIVAL LONDON 81.

We're supposed to play this game: I hide, you find me. And somehow it ends up that Guru Maharaj Ji starts looking for everybody. Then a standstill. Wait a minute, the other way round. Now you look for me. You find me...

The high-pitched voice cuts in again. 'You have a missing piece,' it says. 'You need to change or find it, you must work harder, better.' Loop, loop.

'Only I can give you the peace you need. Reality is an illusion. You are in a relationship with Maharaj Ji forever and you do not exist without him, you have no self beyond him.'

It continues: 'Spy. Listen. Provvy woman's caught up with us already so shh when she's knocking at the door.'

Bill, who has been here all afternoon, laughs. He's staring at an avocado tree he got going himself from the seed that looked like a stone. 'Don't be afraid of the bogeyman, John,' he says, rubbing my dad's hair. 'Debt collector. What a shit job.'

He turns around and watches me as I move into the kitchen.

'Let me ask you this, though,' Bill says. 'If you're working for the man, for the trains, can you always meditate? I mean, like, always?' Bill cradles the little avocado tree near him, touching the brown stem. It has four leaves.

'No, not really… but… come on…' Dad scratches at his beard. Dad has black curly hair and bright blue eyes. When he lets his beard grow, it is hot, bright ginger. My hair is red too, but less intense.

'When I was in Denver,' Bill says, 'everyone took a menial job so that they could concentrate on the breath. If it's repetitive it's better actually. That way you can get to expanded consciousness, right?'

Dad grabs toast from the grill and pulls off the lid of the margarine. Bill fiddles apart Golden Virginia strands and arranges them on a cigarette paper. 'Brakeman is probably pretty repetitive, Bill, you know,' Dad says, scraping margarine on the toast. 'But I'll be like Kerouac, man, the whole dumb saint bodhisattva.'

Bill says, 'You really think it'll be that way?'

'Why not? Walking in the footsteps of Siddhartha, right? Hobo on the rails.'

'I'm just putting it out there, the question: are you sure it's the right job for you? It's all a big industrial fight now anyway, right? Thatcher's fangy little teeth into the rails. Soon all the robots will be shot anyway. Coal's dead.'

I watch Dad get his angry face under control and push it down and away. Toast. Tea. The news makes them shout.

Round and round on my bike. Up the kerb. Back again.

Our new house is further away from Nana's now. The walk takes us through the cemetery. We always go, whenever Mum's not working. Dad has shifts in the packing factory. Nana behind the bar at the Royal Scot. It's all work-work-work, I hear them say in the kitchen. The cemetery is conkers, sycamore, leaf-kicking.

'What are nearly dead people like?' I ask Mum. She talks about death like it's the washing-up. She has a theory that the old people she nurses to their deaths come back as birds who speak to her, thanking her for her time and help. Magpies, sparrows, blackbirds. She is always going to funerals. The next day she calls out to a robin or a pigeon, 'Look, it's Eileen, hello. Yes. Good. Glad it's all right. Glad you're doing okay.'

It is blowy but not yet cold. 'Some want to tell you their secrets or they get very rude and loud at the end,' she says.

Once, she forgot to take her dinner to work, so we took it to her in a carrier bag. She came to the door in her uniform, her hair scraped up under a net. I begged to go in so I could see what a hundred-year-old person looked like, and she let me peek into the room at the skeleton person in the bed and it – death – came all through me and made me feel sick. Guru says when the body is old the soul wants to get rid of it and the problems will be over. New body, new feathers, new wings.

'Do they cry?' Dave says, snot as always free-flowing from his nose.

'Lots.'

'What secrets do they tell you?' I ask.

'Oh, things they regret. The money they've stolen. Sisters they haven't spoken to for fifty years. Dads they hate. Husbands they hate. What they did in the war.'

'What did they do in the war?' We both want to know, but she doesn't answer.

'What do the birds say about being dead?' I ask. I read her face to see what mood she is in. She is always looking up, away, at the sky, into the light. She is tense today and thinking of other things. Her eyes move quickly left and right, and she has smoked three rollies on the walk so far. Other times she is flat and silent. Or she can be alive, talking non-stop.

'The birds just tell me it's going to be okay, it's all okay. Death is nothing to be frightened of.' She's fed up with talking to us now.

'Was Oscar once an old person?' He's our blue canary. My Uncle Gordon came back from being in the army in Berlin and gave him to us as a present. I feed Oscar peas.

'Maybe.' She's fed up with me, I can tell. Shut up, Sue, go away.

Dave runs ahead, picking up the sycamore leaves and helicoptering them. 'Weeeeooouuuuwwwweeeee,' he shouts.

'Why do the old people always give you things?' I ask. She comes home with carrier bags. Bibles. One time, a tiny pocket diary with a four-leaf clover in it. Celebration chocolates. Wine.

'Because they are dying. What's the point? What's the point of holding on to anything that's stuff, that's made of paper or plastic, right?' Her face changes, really really she wants me to shut up. This always makes me talk more.

'I would like to speak bird language,' I say. 'I feel sure I could manage it if I could only be given the secret key. I have a headache and can't be bothered to walk.' I stand still. I have been having trouble with my eyes, and I rub them.

'Come on, Sue.'

'No. Head hurts.'

Dave is far up the path, still helicoptering. Mum stands in the path, irritated with me, her face tight and not smiling. I shiver now the sun has disappeared. We haven't brought our coats.

'Take ten really deep breaths,' she says. 'That usually helps heads.'

I open and close my mouth like a hungry fish. 'No,' I say. 'Boring.'

'It helps you flood with peace. Do it,' she says, voice sharp and angry.

'I'm flooded with hate.' I kick the dirt on the path.

Mum moves away from me. I watch as she walks towards what Dad calls the vanishing point when we draw. The sky is dark, and without warning it starts to rain. Dead people slosh in their coffins, and their birds shake raindrops from their wings. The only shelter is the horse chestnut tree. Dave and I squeeze as close as we can to its trunk.

'Mum, get out of the rain,' I shout, but she won't move. Her neck very straight, arms still by her side. Knitted jumper sagging, her hair stuck to her face.

'I can't,' she says.

'It's easy,' I say. 'You just step here, to the tree.'

Mum puts her face in her hands, and her shoulders shake.

'She's crying,' Dave whispers.

She stands there. 'Lost… lost… lost…' she says.

I'm alert. 'I can help you,' I say, moving towards her. I am focused and strong in my fingers, ready.

'Shut up, Sue. Just shut up for once,' she says. I suspect Dave's crying too, but he's doing it quietly. We are all still. Her eyes are closed, she is getting wetter and wetter in the rain. A railway line runs along the side of the cemetery, and she points to the hedge and the fence. 'I could just go there, couldn't I?' she says to us, but really to me specifically. Her eyes are focused now. 'I could just lie on the tracks and let the train come and that would be better for you, wouldn't it? You'd both prefer it if I wasn't here, wouldn't you?'

I hold Dave's hand, and we look at the floor. Her words are heavy, and we don't know where to put them in our ears, in our heads. I tense my body, look at the horse chestnut cases unzipping and the slimy, shiny nuts getting ready to be thrown.

'Just like that,' she says. 'I'd be gone, and you'd be better.' She walks away from us, but not to the railway tracks, up the path.

'Where is she going?' Dave says. I shush him. My ears are clear and I'm listening for a train in case she runs for it. One of Dave's favourite cartoons is *Tom and Jerry*. I think of the one where Tom the cat ties Jerry to the tracks of a toy railway set. Tom rides, whooping and cheering, on top of the train as it speeds up towards a praying, trapped Jerry. Luckily, Tweety Bird grabs a handy bomb from a toy shelf nearby, flies overhead and drops it on the tracks, just in time. Boom!

We follow Mum, along the path, the rain's gone off a bit now. Not too close. Creep and quiet. I am her protector, like Tweety Bird.

'Imagine,' she says out loud, like she's throwing something over her shoulder. 'I don't think you'd even miss me.'

She doesn't look back, but now she is taking the normal path to the cemetery gate, which leads to Nana's, the way we know off by heart. Every step away from the railway tracks is a good one, I think. Dave's teeth chatter. I watch her light a cigarette, which usually means it's over.

She looks us in the eye and speaks when we get to Birch Avenue. 'We should have brought the coats, shouldn't we?' A weak, unreal smile and a list in my head. I need to draw a map in case she gets lost again. It's my job to remember the coats.

I watch the clock at Nana's. I watch the news. Words I hear a lot: IRA. Miners. Strikes. I sit concentrating on the flowery-covered sofa with my toes too near the gas fire. I'm surrounded by doilies and picture frames. I drink sugary tea, eat crackers with butter, watch the horse racing with Grandad Paddy before he goes to the Butcher's Arms, before Nana goes to the Royal Scot. Before the inky-black time returns, and we are left again with Mum and her thoughts.

Saturday. Things gone. Winnie-the-Pooh pencil case. Disney binoculars. Barbie has no left arm. Plastic horse. Plastic anteater.

She comes in, flops on the chair near the fireplace. 'I'm sorry, Sue. Oscar got out. I left a window open.'

I open the back door and stand in the backyard, but I only see normal brown birds on telegraph wires. I cry. She cries, and Dave. We are all at it. Like this, tears pouring out of us all, turning in circles in the hallway. No one to hook us out of it until Dad gets home.

Dad comes through the door with his friend Sam, one of the Premies. They shake rain everywhere, and before they can speak, Mum pushes past and rushes out the door. She is wearing just her jeans and jumper.

'Muuuum,' I shout, running after her in the street, though I am just in my socks. 'I've got your coat.'

But she's already turned the corner. I go back inside, and Dad and Sam are giggling, shoving biscuits into their mouths. Behind me on the wall is a framed photograph of the five Divine Light Mission commandments (*Don't put off till tomorrow what you can do today! Constantly meditate! Leave no room in your mind for doubt! Always have faith in Maharaj Ji! Never delay in attending satsang!*). I knock it slightly.

'Steady, little lady,' Sam says. He's thin and moves quickly. His eyes dart about. Smoke fills the room and he straightens the picture.

'You need dinner, I guess?' Dad says to me and Dave. For some reason, he thinks this is hilarious. Dad and Sam start banging kitchen cupboards open and closed. 'Let's see, let's see…' they shout.

I stay in the hall to wait for Mum and focus on the commandments. I pick Number Three, *Leave no room in your mind for doubt.* I will repeat it until she comes back.

'Draw the breath in and down and hold it,' the teacher says, looming over us in her bright green Lycra bodysuit. Mum is younger, thinner and cooler than the rest of the women, this much I can tell. The yoga class is in a church hall because they've finally convinced them, Mum says, that it isn't an Eastern form of devil worship.

I hold my breath and suck in my stomach. Maharaj Ji songs in my head, *O Maharaj Ji you are my mother you are my father you are my lover you are all,* and then because I am thinking about it too much, I forget how to breathe and start to cough.

My mum's face is flat and retreating. She does not like to be looked at, especially by other women.

'Roll to your right and sit up,' the teacher says, and thinking I am being told off, I cry. 'It's not really for children, this class, it's too distracting for serious practitioners.' She looks at me, but it's my mum she is talking to.

There is something else. The women in their shiny leotards are from Cheshire villages – Nantwich, Alsager – whereas we are from Crewe. I am cold, sitting cross-legged on the floor, rubbing at the skin on my cheek.

My mum's voice cracks through her shyness. 'You could be kinder,' she says.

The teacher shakes her head. 'This is powerful stuff. Not for kids.'

Mum's lip is shaking. Her hands are too. The entire room watches as my mum shakily pulls up her dungarees, and I understand that we are banished. Outside, on the step, I try to hug her for defending me, but she shakes me off. She flicks my hand away from trying to hold hers and is silent our entire walk home. The red glow of her cigarette tip moves up and down to her mouth. I trail behind her, scuffing my shoes along the kerb, letting damp end-of-summer leaves stick to my toe.

When we reach our house, she goes inside without bothering to look back at me. I stay out and sit on our gate, rocking it backwards and forwards. It is late summer. A cluster of midges hangs around my head. School will start again soon. Our estate has a closed-down feeling. There are a few kids on BMXs at the end of the road, a couple of dogs scratching around a lamp post, but nothing much going on.

Balancing on the gate, I hear a scratchy noise. I twist around and see creatures scampering on the roof of our council house: green and grey, hopping about. They pick tiles from the roof and throw them into the garden, cackling. One of them climbs halfway down a drainpipe and pokes its finger into the dust between the bricks and scrapes as if wanting to dislodge individual bricks from the wall of our house.

Then the creatures grow still and serious and look at me. They are squatting in the gutter of the roof. They blow, puckering little mouths, puffing breath in my direction. At first I think it is kissing, but then I hear the yoga and meditation instructions: breathe in, breathe out, control, pranayama.

Sahita Kumbhaka. Awaken the spine.

I don't want to show fear. I hold on to the gate tighter as a transmission of thought comes from them to me.

Telepathy: 'You can't stop us.' Maharaj Ji's face, familiar to me from the shrines in our house, flits over theirs. Then the faces of the Premies ripple over them too. I shiver, even though it's warm. I swallow their vapours and feel my throat closing. I'm breathless again and my lungs constrict. Their cackling laughter is close.

My mum is at the door. 'Come on in,' she says. 'Bedtime now.'

Her long hair is down, and she looks more relaxed. She doesn't seem to notice the creatures, but I think that is because they are now inside me. They scratch on the lining of my oesophagus; their teeth nibble my stomach lining.

'Sue, are you okay? Sue, do you need your inhaler?' And she runs forward to catch me as I am coughing and falling, but she trips on the step or a gremlin-thing, and I can't tell if I'm catching her or she's catching me. 'Are you okay?'

When I spy, I hear them.

'Satsang, your turn.'

'Well, you pay what you can.'

'It's tight, though, Bill, this month. Money is tight.'

'You know how it goes, Lynda, it's part of the service. Part of love. What is money if not energy? And where do you want that energy to go?'

The book they love is called the *Whole Earth Catalog*, and they have been waiting and waiting for it. It has come from San Francisco.

'SAN FRAN-CIS-CO!' I say. Dad and Bill read it over and over. They dream over it; they smoke and stroke and study it. I lean over their shoulders.

Bill and Dad, fingers running along the index. Aerial photographs. Civilization. Water care. Chainsaws. Seeds. Cannabis. Insulation. Fitness. Hot tubs. Soy food.

But it's the houses they talk about. Owner-built houses, think of it. 'That's the dream,' they say. 'Wooden frame and no fucking rent to pay no fucking landlords. Freedom is land,' they say. Right to buy. This is what I keep hearing. On the news, in the world. I ask them what it means.

Bill turns to me. I can't tell if he's angry. He stands up, leaning over me. Spit comes out of his mouth. 'Right to buy!' he shouts. 'I'll tell you what it is, Sue, it's a great big fucking lie. It's a con. Houses that were meant for everyone are being sold off to greedy piggies. It stinks like rotten fish.'

I have no idea what to say to this. Dad touches my hair, smiles. He says, 'A welding machine, that's what I want.'

When I can get to it, I look at the pictures. Spaceship Earth. Domes and pods. Nests and combs and tunnels and caves. Animal homes, like a wasp nest, like a bird's nest. Irrigation and ventilation. I read: *The mysterious interconnection of things.*

A home belongs in an ecosystem. A home is on earth and earth is an ecology. A home is a nest in the heart of the ecosystem of everything. It is not separate. It is part of the whole. I read it. I pull my new typewriter out on to the kitchen table and start copying the catalogue list. I can see why they like it. It's a catalogue of everything in the world.

'Tools have feelings!' Dad says.

Fingers on the keys, pushing down, clang, bang, kerchunk. I type out the first line from the catalogue. We are as gods and might as well get good at it.

Cassette Player

The Premies had a smell. Grass, damp, patchouli, weed and something else. Lack of deodorant, musk, a hint of mints. What was the other ingredient, the other bit they smelled of?

Before I called Colin Storrs, I flicked through my notebook. I'd been jotting down memories for a few weeks. I'd also been compiling information on the Divine Light Mission. What was I looking for? Hard to say.

Premies. Houses. Ashram. Garden. Always building something: greenhouse, shed, geodesic dome, or welding bits of metal to the back of vans and cars that really should be scrapped.

Bill often hummed 'Suzanne', the Leonard Cohen song I was named after.

The Premies had a particular way of talking that was soft and annoying. When they meditated, they sat under blankets and made a humming noise, oooohhhhhhmmmm, and looked like *Scooby-Doo* ghosts.

A message chat on the forum pinged.

Yes. I know Bill. Yes.

Your parents, I know them.

Yes.

I was at the desk in my university office. I'd put out feelers into the cavernous dark holes of the internet under a sketchy online handle, 'DLMResearcherWriter' and a particular forum was proving lively. I heard the slam of a toilet door a floor above. It was late in the afternoon, a bright day, and we were tipping into the new, busy term. I blinked at my computer screen.

Then: *Yes, Suzanne, I remember you.* Someone called 'the Led' knew my first name.

You do? I typed back.

Red hair. Always hanging around and reading? He private-messaged me his phone number: *I'll be happy to answer questions. Colin Storrs.*

It's for research, I said, though he hadn't asked. He wouldn't give me an email; I had to call.

I googled Colin Storrs for fifteen minutes but came up with nothing. The few people I'd spoken to on the forum so far all had the same story: young, lost, hating parents, needing more, wanting bliss, Guruji took everything, left destitute. Later, they felt like idiots. It was embarrassing, although a part of them still felt special, and sometimes they admitted to missing it all. Now they had no mort-gage, career or pension. He had taken it all. I wanted to ask them: but did it leave you… wanting to die? But that was too heavy. It was an unfathomable question. I wanted to ask: do you mind that he has eradicated the archives? Wiped you out of existence? But that was hard to ask, too.

In the back of my yellow A5 notebook, I'd taken down some basic research on Prem Rawat. I looked through it before I called Colin Storrs. Maharaj Ji, born Prem Rawat, was fourteen when he came to England for the first time, appearing at the second ever Glastonbury Festival in 1971 billed as 'GOD'.

It's possible to watch the footage on YouTube. A grainy night. A flower-covered Rolls-Royce pulls up near the Pyramid Stage. A chubby-faced, nervous-looking Indian boy in a white suit with a teenage shadow-moustache on his top lip is escorted on to the stage. Hari Krishnas and evangelical Christians have formed an unlikely bond against him and shout protests.

Glastonbury was a tiny affair compared to today's beast, a scattering of tents, and no one knew who Maharaj Ji was. Probably the organizer Michael Eavis had confused him with the Beatles' Maharishi. 'Every material thing is perishable!' the Indian teenager shouted to a crowd that had been happily dancing to the Brinsley Schwarz band and now stood frowning at the child-sized guru. 'I have got that thing and I can say you all that I can help mankind and everybody of you by giving that Knowledge…'

Maharaj Ji's accent was strong, and that, coupled with sound tech troubles, meant that the crowd were confused. The teenager then asked the stoned festivalgoers for money, or at least conflated the giving of money with receiving Knowledge. He also told them not to take drugs. Booing began. The mic was cut off by singer-songwriter Nick Lowe, and Maharaj Ji was rushed back into a Rolls-Royce by a team of doting Americans. On the video clip, it's possible to see, as he's urged back into the car, an odd look on his teenage face. Humiliation, or perhaps loneliness. I guess it's lonely being a guru.

Even though he had demanded that everything be destroyed out there, some ephemera from that time could be found. On eBay, for instance, I could buy postcards of people kissing Maharaj Ji's feet. Or press photos from his tours.

Finally, it was quiet in the corridors. I picked up the phone. There is a correlation then, I thought, between people who joined cults and people who didn't seem to mind talking to random strangers from the internet.

He began fast. Perhaps he'd been waiting all his life for this phone call. 'Brothers got me into it. Searchers, seekers, hippies. Drugs, Suzanne. LSD and hash. My brother said: "You don't need anything else in life." He was more hardcore than me. Meditating and listening to the tapes six, seven hours a day.' He stopped. 'I couldn't go to Glastonbury because I had a new baby.' Then he said, 'Do you have a lover, Suzanne?'

'I'm sorry, what?' He repeated the question, and there was a long pause.

He said it again. 'A lover?' He was like a fish monster I'd hooked up from a reservoir of my past, wriggling and on the floor in front of me. I felt disjointed, soiled even. I had no idea what to do with him.

'I don't see…' I moved my phone to my other hand. It felt hot in my palm. My mouth was dry.

'You want to shower a lover with gifts, right? Give them everything,' he said. 'I thought you were going to ask me about money.'

'Well...'

'I vetted your parents,' he said. 'And I had strong reservations, about your mum in particular. But Bill overrode me.'

'Where is Bill now?' I asked, shocked to hear his name spoken so casually in the contemporary daylight. There was a rustling sound at his end. Vet is a nasty little word, I thought, but he ignored my question and switched to the old phrases.

'You can only truly understand Maharaj Ji... I still call him that, I know I'm not supposed to any more, but old habits, you know... you can only get him, his message and his teachings by experiencing his love, Suzanne. You can't be intellectual about it. Or think too much. It's about love, not questions.'

As he said this a snatch of a song – or chant – floated through my head: *Do you wanna become rich? I can make you the richest possible man... Mind you, I don't have the currency of dollars or pounds. I have the perfect currency, which is called Knowledge.*

Students filed along the campus path outside carrying book-filled backpacks, skateboards and bulky black instrument cases. I wished I hadn't called him from my office. It had taken me decades to acquire a room of my own like this. I'd read a million books and published two of my own. I wrote papers and taught writing. My occupancy, and the legitimacy of my residency, derived entirely from letters and ink. Now the sealed edges to my private room were being picked apart by this familiar yet not-familiar voice of Colin Storrs, whoever he was, and the phrases I remembered from the tapes.

People who look for peace get it! That felt like a threat. I lifted my feet from the floor and put them down again. He was an idiot; Maharaj Ji was an idiot. He didn't exist any more, or rather Prem Rawat had rebranded himself. Still, I was unnerved.

People who sit in their houses don't get it.

Knowledge isn't like a programme that is going to appear on television.

Knowledge isn't like a letter that the postman will deliver to you in your home.

You can't get it by relaxing and doing nothing.

'Are you happy, Suzanne?' Colin Storrs said. His voice was soft, whispery. I knew it was the old questionnaire trick, similar to the one used by Scientologists (my parents had been rejected by the Scientologists at a meeting in Manchester when the organizer realized that they didn't have any money).

'Yes, I am happy, thank you. Are you?' I pushed hair out of my eyes and my glasses further up my nose.

'I'm not surprised you've come back to us, that you're reaching out,' he said. 'I always thought you might. There was something special about you when you were little. You had a ray. We all noticed it. You were golden. Special. Your hair, red, rich-coloured, and your cleverness.'

I closed my eyes, pushed my chair back from the desk. 'Well, I'm not reaching out, or coming back.'

'It seems like you are,' he said.

I was hovering around a memory, an internal landscape
that was part of my collective past with my parents but out
of sync with who I was now. It was slimy somehow. There
was an imprint that couldn't be erased, yet conversely was
no longer in existence. A lost archive. I tried to remember
this man who was talking to me, but I couldn't. All I could
see was Bill. Or my dad.

More words from the tapes came into my head, clearly:
*Before you do even approach anybody about this Knowledge, I
request you to do one thing. Look within inside of you, in your
heart, and see if you do have a missing link… the missing piece.
You can find some missing peace.*

'Did you say you know Bill?' I asked.

I heard him say, 'I know Bill, yes.'

'Do you have his number?'

'I can't give you that, I'm afraid, but I'll tell him that you
called at our next major sponsors' meeting.'

'Thank you, Colin,' I said. 'It's kind of you.' I heard my
voice, robotic and cool. He continued talking, sayings from
the tapes converging with those in my mind.

I think I hung up, or he did, and I stopped recording. I
pulled my chair away from my desk, grabbed the metal bin
near the window and was sick into it. When I was done, I
swilled water from my bottle around my mouth and wrote
What a weird reaction in my notebook, even though my hand
was shaking.

A text pinged in. A delivery had arrived at home. It was
a 'job lot' of cassettes from the Divine Light Mission that I'd
found on eBay. When I'd told my husband I'd bought them,

he'd stood leaning against the door frame, filling it with his large, kind body. 'What did you do that for?' he asked. 'I thought you said they creeped you out?'

'They do.'

'Well, why are you bringing them back into your life?'

I couldn't explain. I glanced at my phone to see if Colin Storrs had called me back, but he hadn't. I decided to listen on my iPad to the conversation we'd just had.

We tried to meditate for six, seven hours a day in the early days. It's not easy to sit still, quiet, in your mind for that long, Suzanne. It is extremely challenging.

I'd read that William Burroughs believed a curse could be put on somewhere through 'playback'. This was when he took a recording of a place or time and replayed it at a low level *in situ*. Famously, he'd returned to a cafe where the service had been unsatisfactory and played back his recording to magically jinx the place. I believed, somehow, in the power of bad energy and bad intent. Curses come from a sinister pulse. I had an esoteric, private idea that if I played back the words that had imprinted in my head all those years ago, I might be able to reverse them. Wipe them, even. But, having spoken to Colin Storrs, I now wasn't so sure. Is brainwashing a type of curse?

My notebook was still in front of me. I flicked it open. On an earlier page, I'd written: *My neurons are invaded by the intruders, the Guru or the gremlins, squatting in my neurological pathways. He, or it, or they, or them, reside in the plastic residues of my synaptically connected neuronal assemblies, in other words, my memory banks, forever.*

I walked around campus a few times to get rid of the flavour of the phone call. Out on to the cricket pavilion field,
scraping my September boots on the grass, I made plans in
my head that did not involve looking at sad, old stories. A
trip. A walk. A drive. A shopping list. An afternoon of films
and drawing with my daughter.

Later, at home, I shoved the cassettes from eBay under
my bed, but in the night, I woke up and moved them to the
cupboard under the stairs and away from the edges of my
dreams.

Council House, 1980

Nana disapproves of the fermenting lentils, the lapsang souchong that smells like campfire water, the shrine of Maharaj Ji decorated with wilting daisy chains. I am cross-legged on the floor, half reading, half talking to Nana. Dave's shoving tangerines into his mouth and watching silent cartoons on the telly, which has been turned down in honour of the visitor. Nana is tutting because I said I knew where her secret stash was. I'd found whisky and wine under the blankets in the ottoman, hidden from Grandad Paddy. Mum comes in, stinking of patchouli, sweat patches under her armpits.

'Sue's got something she wants to share with you,' she says.

I look up. My mum is in the door frame, holding my diary. WH Smith, blue with gold lettering. No key. Kept under my bed. Totally private, unhindered thoughts. In fact, a new thing has started to happen to me: I can't stop writing. As if the words are going faster than the pen. I write until my fingers ache, creating a callus on my finger joint. I wear out pencils and make maps with keys and grids. Plans of my road, our estate, leading down into the new Barratt houses, then beyond to the fields and woods. Shops, Ladbrokes, park, rec, bunker, stream. I am figuring out how to get to their sanctuary, where the kids are not allowed to go. My diary is full of this. Mum holds it open and flat, as if it's a plate of biscuits to be eaten by everyone. The curl of a voice, in the air or in my head, picks me up; it is the central authority, the heart of the rules. This is where you finish, it says, this is where you end, and I am smashed open with the private words taken apart and offered up.

'Oh?' says Nana. 'What's that then?'

'It's written here.' Mum reads out a little catalogue of fears. *I think that Nana loves Dave more than me.*

Nana's face is flushed, which is not like her. I am embarrassed because I can tell that my secret fear is true. Dave looks up, confused as he hasn't been listening. Nana folds her hands on her knees. 'Of course I don't. Don't be silly, Sue.'

I run out of the room and up to my bedroom and slam the door. Mum is on the stairs, shouting, 'Ashima and truth are the central conducts…' I scan my room. The tips of my fingers are very hot. I open a pack of felt-tip pens. I write every swear word I know, which is all of them, on the back of the door. I refuse to come out. She does not respect my wishes. If I said go away, she would sit on top of me. If I said come here, she would walk away. I have a ringing in my ears and a fury that makes my bones want to come out through my skin. Even though I don't want her to, she is in the room. She sits on the edge of the bed with a white face and thin lips.

'Why did you read my diary, and why did you read it out to Nana?'

She says: 'Maharaj Ji's teachings say to bring up the weight of our secret fears, put them on the table and end the suffering. Then you don't have to be controlled by things that cause you pain. If you bring it out, it heals. That's what I was trying to do.'

'You aren't even sorry?'

'You take the black, ugly, shameful, disgusting bits of yourself and you put them out into the bright sunlight.' She stands up and goes over to my pile of books against the wall.

'I don't think I have black shameful bits inside me,' I say.

Mum looks at the floor. Up at the ceiling, anywhere but me. Her eyes move around, fast left and right. 'I think it's weird that you've never liked dolls,' she says, standing up suddenly.

I don't know what to say; I don't know what logic I'm dealing with. The anger disappears and I am very close to crying, but I keep it in.

'Everyone has shameful bits,' she says.

I sit on the floor for a while when she's gone, trying to think about nothing. I pick up a glass jar of marbles that I won at the school fair. A pickled onion jar filled with the blue swirly cat-eye marbles that come in a red string bag. I hold it up in the air and count to ten. Every part of me is rushing, sweating, prickling. I let it drop on to the floorboards, hoping for a smash of glass. And blood and dripping pain on the walls. And a crushing, echoing breaking of existence as exemplified by marbles. But the jar rolls on the carpet and about half of the marbles scatter.

Later in the living room, my diary is on the table near a lamp for anyone who cares to look. I throw it into the coal fire. I don't know what my mum read. The thing about Nana wasn't a deep, painful secret anyway, just a stupid little fear, but it was private. I think I see the letters A K C P S Q J I Q A C P evaporating into the coal and smoke, each one letting out a squeak before disappearing. I cannot trust paper, ink, pages, books, secrets, lies or hidden diaries. What I need is invisible ink. But it occurs to me that what I'm upset about the most is that she read it and still didn't see my secrets.

'Who the fuck are all those people trooping in and out of yours, Suzanne?' Gemma's mum wears mascara that is bright green or blue and clogs in the corner of her eyes. I run my hand along the VHS tapes piled in the hall and read their titles: *A Wild and Wet Weekend*, *A Special Visit* and *Lick Lucy*. She often walks around their house naked and unbothered by my presence. I am an estate brat to her, but now and then she eyeballs me. 'Who are they?' she repeats.

'Friends,' I say, blushing. She stubs out her cigarette on an uneaten piece of toast and laughs. Her body is tiny but extremely curvy, like a drawing of a woman that goes bloop-breasts, shrink-waist, bloop-hips. When she stretched her arms up I noticed a long vertical scar on her belly. She's had seven children and two babies who didn't make it, so she can't be that young, though I think she started early. Premies won't have TVs in the house, so I hang around here to watch *Dynasty* and learn about affairs, drinking and back-stabbing.

Gemma's elder sister, whose legs don't work, drags herself across the carpet in nappies that remain unchanged for hours. I sit on their stairs and count the animals. Rangy cats, sad-eyed dogs and a balding chinchilla that is occasionally let out of its cage. The pets are fed from tins on the floor and the kids from tins on the table. There are broken toys everywhere and piles of clothes on every surface, but I like it here. It smells of old weather and damp tea towels. No one is working towards Knowledge.

I lurk in the door frame of the kitchen, waiting. Today's the day for the Altrincham skating rink. When I'd asked my parents if I could go along, they weren't sure. Mum said, 'She pumps the kids out to keep the benefits rolling in.' Bill said, 'That's one way of screwing the system, I guess.' Dad said, 'Ice skating, cool.'

Gemma carries a rucksack on her back everywhere she goes because she likes the feeling of being weighed down. Without it, she says, she has a sense that she is sitting on the top of a pole and can't balance or get still. She is the only other human, outside of my family, that I care about. In some ways she is more than a person; she is a place, a hope.

Gemma and I are self-taught skaters, passionate about technique. Don't stand too upright. Bend knees, weight on the balls of feet. Tummy in, shoulders forward. Heave forward with toes out until you glide. To stop: feet parallel, then heels outward. Knees bent, body upright.

Skating is a rush, a dream.

We circle the circumference of the rink as fast as we can, fearless and white-whipped with ice air. We skate backwards, fast, weaving legs in and out. The icy rink smells of chips frying in the cafe. There is an explosion of screaming kids, shouts, booming music and bleeps from the arcades. On the ice, I am in a roofless sky. I am in an ocean library. A silk doorway. A lost river. When I glide, the hands of the clock fall away and I spin in timeless space, in perfect sequence with Gemma. We float close, touch hands, glide away.

Mickey leans on the railing, smiling as we whizz past. 'Faster, girls,' he shouts. 'Go, go, go.' He is a skinny, gawky man and his tongue is coated in yellow stuff. He sucks on Marlboro Reds as he watches us. He drives us there, gets us the tickets and pays for lunch. He even bought us skating skirts and leotards from the skate shop. Gemma's is sky blue, mine peach with white sequins. The flared parts of our skirts come up as we twirl. When I've mastered the turns, it's as though I might float up, corkscrewing to the clouds.

When our session is up, I tug the yellow paper bracelets off my wrist and bend down to unclip the hired skating boots. Gemma is opposite me on an ice-damp plastic chair, tugging at her own boots.

Mickey lopes towards us. 'Fun?'

'Yeah,' I say.

'You're a good little skater,' he says to me, his Adam's apple bobbing up and down. 'Like a…' I look up, waiting to find out what I am like.

'I don't know.' He stares. 'Can't think. You remind me of one of those little dolls that pops up out of a jewellery box, you know what I mean?'

Gemma's eyes narrow. 'Ballerina?' she says.

'That's it. You look like a spinning ballerina.' He smiles at me, creased face. Sunken cheekbones.

Gemma pulls chewing gum from her mouth and sticks it under her chair. 'Ballerinas are completely different from skaters.'

Mickey sniffs. 'Chips, girls?'

Later, when she goes to the toilet, I am looking up at the window of the shop at the rink. White ice skates hang on a home-made tree with tinfoil wrapped around the branches. The blade of the boot has an engraved swirl design. The corrugated tip shines.

'Put them on your Christmas list?' Mickey says, standing near me.

'Yeah,' I say, embarrassed that it is so obvious that I want them. He puts his hand on my neck and squeezes it a little, for one second. His fingers under my hair are cold.

'Hey,' he says, 'so those freaks you live with?' He pulls his hand away.

'What?'

'I've seen them all coming to your house. Weirdo-freaks in the sandals and the stupid coats.'

'Yes.'

He leans close, his breath near the back of my ear. 'I don't like them. Shitty types. If you have trouble with them, any of them, you come and tell me now, okay?'

'Trouble?' I say. 'They are... they are okay.' I put the tip of my ponytail into my mouth and chew it.

Again the tips of cold fingers on my neck; this time the squeeze is harder. He tugs me as if he is about to hang me up on a washing line. 'No, they aren't okay. They are disgusting losers. Any shit from any of them, just come across the road to me, okay?'

I nod.

'I'm not far, am I?' he says. 'Just over the road.' When he drives us home and speaks, little bits of spit fly out of the window or occasionally back towards me. I wipe them off my face with the palm of my hand.

Gemma and I go to the rows of pebbledash-clad houses that turn into new Barratt homes. The gardens don't yet have grass, and the road fizzles out into farmland, ditches and the smell of Cheshire muck. We pass a disused shed on the edge of the wood, perhaps once something to do with the Scouts but now abandoned. Inside, hooks on the wall and the smell of old paint, varnish and tarmac. Then it turns into scrubby clearings in the trees, with lots of rubbish on the floor. Boxes, old milk bottles, a lone shoe. Estate kids flit through these woods playing a complex game, some in combat gear and army surplus. A huge ash tree is the meeting point where freckled boys trade penknives, matches and flint. Gemma and I rattle past on our bikes, keeping roughly to the path, bouncing over roots and sticks. A lanky boy follows us. We are fast, but he's climbed up on to the high back as our bikes wobble over the bumpy ground. My bike wheel jams on a tree root, and I come to a stop. I call to Gemma, who's ahead, and she screeches to a stop. He's got something out of his pocket, a sling or a catapult. He bends down then looks at me. Points it right at me. My foot sinks into the soil. I drag my bike forward, towards the bit of the path that leads to a disused sewage works. Stones come firing at me. 'Come on,' Gemma shouts. Stones flying, clods of earth. He shouts, 'Stuck up bitch, weirdo bitch.'

Usually, when I'm with Gemma, the bigger kids don't throw gravel at me or push me off my bike for wearing charity shop dresses instead of Adidas trainers and tracksuits. The uniform includes signet rings and Lacoste t-shirts. There is a specific way of rolling sports socks in this world. Gemma is native, but I am stuck in home-knit jumpers of shame.

This boy, though, I can see he scares her too. We ride off fast, out of the woods and along a lane that leads to the corner of the rec. There is a concrete bunker here. It is graffitied and smells of rat's piss inside, but it is completely private. We call it the Museum because it feels historical, as if it is from the war. We squat inside, facing each other, crouched like waiting spiders. We don't speak for a bit and let our bodies recalibrate. Her eyes are the colour of brown caterpillars, my favourite kind. We are both small, skinny and scab-kneed, but otherwise we are opposites. I have red hair and sunburn easily. She is dark-haired, with golden skin that tans. I am blind – I need glasses, but don't know that yet – and I am clumsy. She is elegant, skilled and powerful. If the nuclear bomb we'd watched on *Threads* was to come, I knew which of us would be gone first.

'Do you know who he is?' I say.

'Not sure. I've seen him. He's an idiot.'

'Why do they all hate me?' I ask, but Gemma just shrugs. At school, she uses her finger to keep to the lines when she reads, but in the world, she explains everything to me and is scared of nothing. She can get a bike chain back on really fast and knows the narrowest bit of the stream to jump. At school, she gives me a mild salute in the corridors, and I understand that she can't be associated with my weirdness in public places.

'Was number two stepdad better than Mickey?'

'Kevin?' She shrugs. 'He was thick. Meant I could get stuff out of him, but he was useless.'

'Right,' I say.

'Mickey isn't thick, unfortunately.'

'No,' I agree. Mickey has eyes like a fox and a brain that zips ahead.

'Mickey really hates your parents,' she says. 'Keeps going on about it. Calls them losers.'

I laugh. 'They *are* losers!' I want to tell her more, but don't know how.

Whenever I tell my parents about kids who consider me a freak at school, they have the same, unhelpful reaction: 'Don't worry, Sue,' they say. 'The conveyor belt of school and work is temporary. This reality is illusory and meaning-less. The kids kicking you in the shins in the playground are irrelevant because they will be left behind in the end. It's all *lila*, remember? Part of the great game, like a carpet tapestry.'

'What are they into?' Gemma asks. 'Are they Christians?' She's never spoken to me directly about them before like this.

'No.' How to explain? 'Meditating, I suppose.' She says nothing.

I don't know why, but I think of my mum's knitting needles. I like the big fat bamboo ones, but she rarely uses them.

'Do you ever think your house is going to crack in half?' I say, watching her as she picks at one of her knee scabs.

'No.' Her calmness is always reassuring.

'I sometimes think my house is going to fall apart, break in two. I keep dreaming about it.'

She sniffs. 'What are you frightened of?'

My mum's face comes to me: when she is taking things from the house and throwing them into a bin liner or moving around in a scary, silent rage. The 'techniques', this is what they talk about in the kitchen. What are they? Sometimes they call them methods. The knitting needles are never thrown away, though. I've noticed that.

'Dunno,' I say. 'They have a secret that I am not allowed to know about, but when they get there, or get it or whatever, it will be magical for them, but me and Dave aren't allowed to be part of it. They are all going somewhere, without us.'

She is looking at me, hard and serious. Then she sighs, rubs the edge of a nostril. 'Going somewhere?'

I shrug. 'It's weird.'

It's not a good idea to talk about this stuff to anyone. I regret having said any of this, even though I trust her.

I think of the map I once drew in class, and the teacher pulling me up on it, asking me to stay behind: 'What's this then, Suzanne?'

One of the Maharaj Ji cassettes tells of a group of specially selected Premies who will soon be called to live under a golden dome called the Sanctuary. The way to the Sanctuary is up a ladder and through an attic. Outside, the whole world will die, and the chosen Premies will step out with Maharaj Ji into a fresh, perfect world called the Infinite. My map has all the elements: Dome. Sanctuary. Attic. Guru. 'That is where my parents are going,' I say. 'But I'll be left behind.'

'Why?'

'Because I don't have the Knowledge. But they do… or they are working towards getting it.'

'What is the Knowledge?'

'I don't know.'

'Why are you left behind?'

'Because children don't go. They are obstructions.' And the look he gave me. Frowned. Like I was shit on his shoe. Then he pretended to care. 'Come to me if you need any-thing, okay?'

Gemma smiles. 'Definitely sounds weird,' she says.

'Remember that homework we had?' I ask. 'The bronchial tree in the lungs. We had to label the separate parts: upper lobe, lingula, lower lobe. Do you remember?'

She screws up her nose. 'Dunno.'

'When I was doing it, I realized that it looked like a crack on the ceiling above my bed, underneath the attic. A sort of Y with splinters coming from it.'

'Yeah,' she says, looking at me with narrow eyes.

'The Y on the ceiling is the same as the one in my lungs, in the bronchial tree, and if I hold my breath I think I can stop the ceiling from cracking and the attic from falling through and I will be protected from them.'

'Who is it?' Gemma asks. 'Who are they? Who are the "them" you want to be protected from?'

But she already knows I don't know either. She's quiet for a minute.

'Well, Mickey wants to turn our attic into a "cinema room". I know what kind of films he likes to watch.'

Words are like the fish in the pond at the park, uncatch-able and slippery. When I lean over the bank and put my hands in the murky green water, the fish disappears.

'Mickey asked me if you want to come ice skating with us,' she says, not looking at me. 'I don't know if it's a good idea though.'

'Why?'

She looks at me. I never asked her why Kevin the second stepdad left. We are both silent. Here are our bones, our ribcages and our brains. We are fragile, made of glass, but we'll grow.

I've never tried ice skating, but I can picture the spinning and flying. A word I read once comes to me: quarry. Hunters. I imagine how it must feel to be picked up by a swooping bird, tugged up with claws and beak, dragged upwards with all my skin and hair. Ice skating will help me to get strong, to escape, surely?

'How can I get rid of the bogeyman?' I say, out of nowhere.

She sits up, interested. Gives it some thought. 'Here are the options. Kill him? Tell your mum about him? Confront him and scare him?'

I think about it. A bogey-shapeshifter; hard to see, harder to catch. Perhaps my dad is friends with the bogeyman?

Perhaps the bogeyman is inside my head? How do I tell my mum?

'Which of those might work?' she says, wanting to know. 'I can tell my dad.'

Gemma sighs and goes back to her scab-picking. 'Good luck with that.' She pulls something out of her pocket. It is a box of matches. She loves fire. She sometimes sits flicking through an entire box of them, spit and fizz and the extinguished smoke. 'Let me know if you need me to burn them all down,' she says, smiling.

Yes. I will. I will.

'Just say the word,' she says. 'I'll be ready.'

And I say to her, 'Let me know if you need me to do the same for you too.'

She scrapes her fingernails into the earth. 'We should draw something, write something, leave a mark,' she says.

'Why?'

'Dunno... maybe one day they'll make this into a museum about us?'

A woman's voice on the phone, high-pitched but not quite a squeak. 'A question, Suzanne: who is your mum in bed with?'

The magnets on the fridge door are *Peanuts* characters: Woodstock, Charlie Brown and Snoopy himself. I stare at the wiggled line that is Charlie Brown's hair. 'Pardon?'

I'm in charge of Dave, getting his milk, getting him to bed, by myself on nights when she goes to yoga (Tuesdays) and some extra-special mediation sessions she takes with Bill (Thursdays). Dad works nights in a new job he's got at the

Marks & Spencer food-packing factory. She'll be back by ten. It is no different to when everyone is in. I am nine, a big girl. I am fine. Often our phone is cut off, but not this time.

The voice again, speaking slowly, so that I will understand and not miss a word. 'I said, ask your mum… when she gets back… who she's been in bed with.'

'Yes,' I say as if I'm replying to a teacher and this conversation is normal. Clock, fridge, the wind coming through the gap in the front door frame. Tap dripping. I look out of the black kitchen window for murderers in the garden, but all I see is my white face and my Garfield t-shirt nightie. On the wall are some pages stuck up with masking tape:

Maharaj Ji is this tree of life, this tree of love.

You have been given this tree of life, of love. This seed.

You should treat this seed, this seed, which is love within you, as the most precious gift that you'll ever receive. Because truly it is, you should guard it with your life.

She isn't back, even though it's twenty past ten. I stand near the phone, wanting to speak to the unsettling voice to have someone to talk to. In my notebook, I write: *Who in bed with? Who on phone?*

I open the front door and look out on to the cold street. October. The parked cars look like sleeping beasts, and the street is different at night. I look over at Gemma's house and think about going over and knocking, but to say what? A phone call? A mum at yoga? I wait, door open, with a notebook and a torch. With the door a bit open behind me, I sit on the step and continue writing. *Tree of life, if I burned it if I burned it. Guard it with your life, guard it with your life.*

'What ya doin', Suzy-Sue?'

I squint up into the darkness. It is Mickey, standing with a motorcycle helmet in his hand, though I hadn't heard his engine. He's like an illustration in a book: black lines, hatched shading and hooded eyes. He smells of something, but I don't know what it is. 'Nothing.'

'Where's your mum and dad?'

'Not here.'

'Left you all alone?'

I stand up. I close the book in my hands and step slightly backwards into my house. His hands are on the gate, then he opens it and comes down the path towards me. His boots have silver caps over his toes. He opens his mouth to say something, and I focus on the aggressive point of his Adam's apple. He is near and smiling. Then very close to me. He puts his finger on my chin, rubs it for a second, and then takes hold of the neck of my Garfield nightie. He leans over me; he fiddles with the fabric and then pulls it away from my skin and peeps down.

'What's in there then?'

I stand very still. A Maharaj Ji passage that's recently been playing a lot comes through my mind:

You have received the shelter and now you are afraid of nothing in this world.

You have received the shelter of such a thing, you are wearing a bulletproof coat, such a coat that even when bullets come to you, they won't harm you. Don't, don't go out of the shelter. Always try to be in the shelter. It is your home. Your house. A museum. A place of sanctuary.

He tugs the top of my t-shirt even further away from my skin and again looks down. My feet are bare and my toes are cold. The noise of a car engine fills the street. It pulls up, tyres twisting on gravel. I recognize the sound. It is Bill's Thunderbird, and then there is a door opening and footsteps and my mum at the gate, swaying a little.

Mickey stands back now with his hands on his hips, making a clicking noise with his mouth. 'There you are,' he says, glaring at them. 'Your daughter was all alone in the street and I was just about to phone the police.'

A bit later, in my room, Mum fiddles with the corner of my pillow. 'Why did you open the front door? Why didn't you just wait for me?' There is a flapping look in her eyes like a lid is going up and down in her head. I tell her what the woman had said on the phone and watch as she bites her bottom lip. 'What?'

I repeat the message and look closely at her face, trying to read it. Her breath is quick and choppy. She picks up my drawing book and flicks through it, but she isn't looking at my drawings. She asks me what time the woman called and what I'd said and did I know who it was. She smells of cigarettes and something else. Not yoga.

'You're good at drawing,' Mum says. 'Like Dad, though you're more doodly.'

'Suppose so.'

'Will you keep a secret?' She taps the bed three times like she's knocking on a door. 'I know you are clever, and I know you can. Will you keep my secret?'

'Depends.'

'I'm depressed,' she says, shaking her head. Looking down, at the bedcovers, down at the floor. 'It will be hard for you to understand. I'm so sad, Sue. I can't stop it. It just comes down to everything all the time. Sometimes I just want to die. To kill myself, you know? I'm working with Bill on the techniques, you see, to get me up and out of it again, but I really don't want to worry Dad. I don't want him to know how sad I am.'

I look at her fingers. 'How can you want to kill yourself when you have Dave and me?' I say, but she doesn't answer that. I look down. My fingers are tracing k-i-l-l on my knees.

'Will you keep it a secret? Me popping out. It's all nothing to worry about. I've just been depressed, but it's getting better now and you keeping this to yourself will help me to… recover.'

'Yes, Mum,' I say, sitting up straight and looking at her eyes, which are bulging. 'Yes, I can keep it a secret.'

The breath comes out in a rush. She rubs her right cheek and looks at me strangely. At the door, she stands and leans on the frame and waits. I can sense her changing. Great big wings, the essence of a bird. A crow, or something scrappy. A beak.

She pushes against the door in an irritated movement as she leaves. 'I don't think you should go over to Gemma's house any more. I don't like that Mickey guy.'

I don't answer that. I can see she is still on the landing. She closes the door and I think: if being a kid has a shape or form, it's a long thin road that is sometimes clear to see and other times thin and bleak with no obvious end, like paper that's been used but not properly thrown away.

*

Geography. When Grandad Paddy goes to the pub, he calls it going to Czechoslovakia. When Dad loses his job on the railways because of too much meditating, he calls it going to Ireland; he goes into his room for weeks.

I write to him on my typewriter, but I don't give him the letters.

The run-up to Ireland is days of fighting between my parents, scraps and yelling, teary voices and low banging. Dave and I make ourselves into nothing. Food comes, we eat it – tomato soup, beans, a bowl of raw salad. They push the plates at us, but they aren't seeing us. We sort ourselves out for bed, brush teeth and find pyjamas. Dave watches VHS tapes of *Star Wars*.

Our bedrooms are whirlwinds of disorder. Sometimes I attempt to create order within it, straightening my bedcovers and arranging my felt-tip pens in a tiny mosaic of structure.

Dad stops speaking completely. He has no voice. My mum talks louder; she is all voice. She comes into our rooms here and there, face blotched with crying. The loud bit lasts three days or so, sometimes four. After the talking, a black mood. Dad only comes out to use the loo. I type it out: *In room 3 hours. In his room 7 hours. Week one. Week two.* I chart it. Mum moves around the house in straight lines, like the endless square angles of an Etch A Sketch. Towards the end of it all, even she has used up all the words and the house is quiet, apart from my typewriter keys.

During this time, I cycle to the bunker on the rec. Sometimes with Gemma, sometimes alone. I draw. A museum of myself. A house-museum. We plan it.

'I know how to make a house,' I say. I tell her about the *Whole Earth Catalog*. I've been reading the house-building pages: how to construct, how to create, how to make a house. In the bunker I start my plans: a house/museum/suitcase.

Gemma says, 'I need that. A catalogue with the tools of everything, how to do everything. How to build something that will get us out of here.'

AUTUMN

The drug I can give is constantly working in you twenty-four hours a day. It's built inside you, it's built-in acid, it works inside you, and it is completely free. The only thing that has to be done is to connect the wire, then it starts working. That's very beautiful because other drugs give you external experience, and this one gives you internal experience.

Maharaj Ji (Prem Rawat), 1977

Suitcase

'I dreamed about the attic again,' I said to my daughter as we walked to school. September. Term time. Pencil cases and shiny, unscuffed shoes. 'There's a suitcase up there, I want to get it down.'

'What's in it?' She was looking in gardens. She preferred talking to cats over humans. My son skipped ahead. I talk to them in a way I don't talk to anyone else, which is to say I tell them the truth. I was thinking about rescue and reparation: how to get my parents out of the trap. I'd had a dream about the suitcase the night before.

'Can't remember,' I said, which was not entirely true. I'd bought it with some birthday money when I was around my son's age, to hide stuff from the purges. I'd held on to it through all these decades. The suitcase had a red sticker on the lid that said MUSEUM. It was a cliché, the kind now used as a prop in Anthropologie store windows and hipster bars. I dragged it for years from university rooms and bad situations until eventually shoving it in my attic.

My son turned back and looked at me, his cheeks bright red. 'Are you afraid to go up there?'

'Not exactly.'

'Is it full of paper?' he asked. He was big now, they both were. Flying through the kitchen, spreading splashes of water and mud. Grunting at me, ignoring me, spontaneously hugging me with hot faces and sweaty hands, opening the fridge door, shouting 'Food!' and then hissing at me from the stairs.

'Yeah.'

He shuddered. They were both digital natives, but it was my son who hated writing. He told me it hurt his fingers and gave him an unwelcome sensation in his hands. A mother of another thirteen-year-old I know tells me that her son can't write. He physically can't do it. He was seeing an occupational therapist every Wednesday morning who made him squeeze Play-Doh to uncramp his fingers. Together we shook our heads and agreed that it was the end of days. The unwriting of boys.

'Hold your pen like this,' I say to my son when we practise at bedtime. 'Don't squeeze it so tight, you're not trying to get blood out of it. You're not trying to write in blood.'

His eyes go wide. 'It would be more fun if it were blood instead of ink.'

'Okay,' I say, 'pretend it is. Black blood, spilling on to the page.'

'Cool.' He prefers keys and screens to paper and who can blame him? 'Paper's for dead people,' he says. 'It gets stuck. You know? Weighs you down. I don't get the point of it.' He agreed to write each night, just a sentence or two about his day, to keep his hands from cramping and his brain from resisting the pincer movement of using a pen. Sometimes I sat with him while the lines of his page filled up, resisting the urge to read his thoughts.

'Did you write your diary last night?' I asked as we walked. He shook his head. 'I'll do you a deal,' I said. He loves to strike a deal, like Rumpelstiltskin. He looked excited, like it might mean he'd get something.

'What?'

'You keep writing on paper if I clear out the ghosts in the attic.' He shrugged.

My daughter swirled round. 'Ghosts?'

'Not real ones,' I said. 'Don't worry.'

My son was not bothered; it didn't sound like the kind of deal that resulted in a prize. For instance, something credible in playground banter-trade where the kid with the most expensive phone was king/queen.

'You crack your fear and I'll crack mine?' He shrugged again. 'All right,' I admitted, 'what I'm saying is, I need your help. Will you help me brave the attic again?'

He puffed up like a juvenile owl on its first hunt. 'Oh. What's up there anyway?'

'Junk,' I said. 'Old stuff that needs to be chucked.'

The kids left me at the school gates and disappeared into the kind of light that makes a day nostalgic while it's already happening.

The suitcase was full of old notebooks, some salvaged diaries, sketchbooks. Disarray and cobweb. As I flicked through the papers, my dad called. I put him on speaker. He was going to Wales for a ten-day silent meditation retreat, he said.

He gave me the contact number as he was not allowed his phone.

A life of factory work, of repeated manual labour, is stamped again and again into the body. Shaking hands. A tremor. A stiffness. A hurting. Tinnitus. Repetitive strain injury and aching into the skeleton. He said the window sashes of his flat were rotten and that he was seriously worried that the panes of glass would come through. That they would smash and he'd be exposed to the elements.

'You need to tell the landlord.'

'Yeah, I will, I will,' he said, in a voice that meant he wouldn't. The only heater he had in his flat was a small electric one that he tried not to use. Sometimes, embarrassed, I offered him money. He always declined.

A story:

Dad was seventeen when he met Mum. She was so shy that she spoke in whispers and hid her face behind curtains of brown hair. She didn't take any of the exams at school. She got accepted on to a nursing course on the condition that she resat a maths test, but she knew, privately, that she would fail.

The house party on the edge of an estate was full of trainee teachers from Alsager College. There were hippies from the Potteries, a group of hashish dealers who worked in a toilet-making factory in Stoke, and students from Keele University who made LSD in the campus lab. 'She was wearing yellow hot pants and was by far the coolest girl in the room, even though she didn't speak,' my dad said. He was sporting a cracked jaw. His dad had thrown a table at his head because he wouldn't cut his hippy hair and was embarrassing him at Rolls-Royce, where my dad was a trainee draughtsman. The plan was this: draughtsman, Rolls-Royce, forty-five years of service, pension. Dad was rebelling.

Smoking joints and drinking warm wine at the party, my dad told my mum a tale because, before this story, there was another story, like matryoshka dolls.

Towards the end of the fifties, my grandad pulled my dad, aged five, out of the car by his wrists and threw him on the gravel, sharp edges pushing into his knees and palms. 'No more sissy stuff.' He hit him across the skull. Not hospital-hard, but enough for a deep, painful ring in the ear. It was a car park on the edge of a beach in Ireland. My grandad was the sort of man who, when he hit his children, liked to do it from behind so they couldn't see it coming. Every one of his children flinched when he came into a room. He crouched down and took my dad's left ear, squeezed it hard and tugged his face close. 'Make your way home. It's only forty miles. If you don't, you know what's coming.' He handed him a paper bag. That morning my Welsh nana had put a ham sandwich and an apple in it, as well as one of the army flasks full of water, and then turned towards the sink. She hadn't said goodbye.

Dad told me that he didn't move at first and that it had taken a minute to realize that he had been left on this beach alone. The sea looked nice, but it was far away. There were no people. This wasn't a popular beach. Seagulls looped and flies buzzed around him; they wouldn't leave him alone.

He had a wee behind a clump of grass then returned to the exact spot he'd left. Finally, the sun went down. He'd drunk the water and eaten the food. His face itched, and he was frightened of the sand bugs that hopped on his feet, like dog fleas but different. When it was completely black, he curled up on the damp sand and let it come around him.

He didn't know what time it was when he heard his dad's boots scrunching on the sand, but it was the morning. The smack he got for failing to be a man caught him on the right side of his skull, followed by a punch in his stomach and ribs. It made him convulse so much that spit came out, but still, my dad was grateful.

This place on the cold sand on the beach in Ireland was a landscape my dad struggled to escape from. Later, he would discover that all the journeys – physical, metaphysical, spiritual, literal – took him back there. Later, he would discover he could never escape the sound of boots crunching on the sand.

'I'm looking through old photos, letters, stuff,' I said to the phone.

I heard him rustle around at the other end. 'Oh yeah? Be careful or you'll start crying into your tea like me. I'm getting sentimental in my old age.'

As he spoke, I picked out a cutting from the *Divine Times*. A picture of Maharaj Ji as a child dressed in Indian regalia and holding a flute against his mouth as if playing it, a mini Pan. It was dated 1982, and here was my eight-year-old self's handwriting on the back: *Maharaj Ji when I was born you were 16. I could be your wife. When I am older, I would like to be your wife. Guru play your flute for me. Perfect knowledge not materialism.* I ran my fingers over the old, faded ink, trying to find my way back to remember that belief in myself. I wanted to ask Dad about Maharaj Ji, or maybe about his dad and that Irish beach. It was Mum who had told me that story. I'd not heard it from him directly. But it was difficult to bring up the Divine Light Mission. Mainly, I think, because he still believed in it, or in something, or in meditation. Or something he considered 'Eastern' and enlightening at least.

He sighed. 'Must be something in the air. I've been thinking about the past too. Do you remember coming on the trains to Carlisle with me?'

I thought. 'No. Don't think so.'

'I guess you were about six.' He told me about when he was working on the freight trains. He'd gone all the way to Carlisle and back. When he was there, he'd had enough time to wander to a bookshop. In there he saw a copy of D.H. Lawrence's *Complete Poems*. It was £5. His salary at that time was £40 a week. He talked himself out of it and travelled back to Crewe. When he came in from his shift, he said to me, 'Want to come on the train with me?' We went back, apparently, just us. I was five. He bought the D.H. Lawrence book, and I chose one too. 'You don't remember, Sue?'

I tried to locate it, the lovely memory of going to Carlisle for books with him, but it wasn't there. I was sad about that. I wished that memory was locked in my head, but it was gone. I felt its lack like a sadness.

'Why did you leave that job, Dad?'

'What? Trains?'

'Yeah.'

'Well…'

I decided to say it, the name from long ago. 'Was it because of Bill?'

'Bill!' he said. He took a long breath. 'Yes, we met Bill and that's when we got introduced to Maharaj Ji, and Bill offered me some work that summer, cash in hand, with him, and so I left it all, the job, the pension, all that bullshit.'

I listened to him slurp more tea. It was the first time I'd heard him say 'Maharaj Ji' for decades. He'd had a stroke a year ago but still went every day to the factory on an industrial estate in Eastbourne that he had worked in for the last twenty years. He was trying to figure out how to retire.

It had been my mum's idea to run away from Crewe. Donovan had famously spent the summer of 1964 in Torquay, washing up in a hotel and busking, and she used to go there as a kid on holidays. The sea, the trinkets, the piers, the promenades, a UK hippy trail for the ones who couldn't hope to get the cash together to go to India or Afghanistan.

David Bowie played Torquay as part of his Ziggy Stardust tour, and the locals weren't shy about hating the hippies. My dad washed glasses, plates, breakfast stuff, soup bowls in a hotel, just like Donovan. Seasonal work was everywhere, but in the winter they holed up in their boarding house room.

I don't know if it was raining when my mum told my dad she was pregnant with me, but, given that it was an English seaside town in the winter, it's likely. Years later, stoned one night when I was a teenager, he told me that he had missed his chance. He was about to leave Lynda. Make a run for it. She was always crying; it was miserable and boring. But then she gave me the news. 'Tricked me.' But then he'd looked at me. 'Thank God she did. I have you!' Tricked.

'Please get the landlord to look at the window, Dad. The wind's freezing.'

Whatever I was looking for wasn't in my suitcase. It was an empty vessel that I had once used to smuggle things out. Artefacts and items were in there, but it was missing crucial information. My archive was extremely faulty. I began to understand the appeal of shoving everything in a bin and setting it on fire. Yet it seemed that even if you tried to destroy things, stuff would make it out. Cuttings, lone photographs and fragments of material would set off on their own voyages, like paper planes. Maybe it wasn't that I wanted to reassemble my archive, but that I wanted to be more thorough in its destruction.

Council House, Early 1980s

'If the beads are on the door' – my mum tips the remains of a packet of Bombay mix into her mouth – 'it means you must be silent. In the house and the front garden.'

Now they have received the Knowledge. From what I can tell they look the same, but they are definitely more secretive. They often disappear into the bedroom.

I hop off the gate and pick up my skipping rope. I've heard Bill say: 'So intense, such a spiritual experience. Nothing matches it. You will be free.' If I skip here, they can't go in or out without me knowing.

In the run-up to getting the Knowledge Dad finally passed his driving test. He sold his record collection to buy a yellow VW Beetle.

Mum kept saying, 'Will they think we are enough?'

Bill: 'You've shown a willingness, Lynda. I'm sure of that.'

Dad kept saying, 'But will we get chosen this time or will it be like last time?'

Bill: 'The darshan destroys a year's karma. Remember that.'

I'd asked my dad what that meant, and he'd said that you lie on the floor near the Master (Ruler) as he walks past and you are allowed to kiss the ground, or if you are lucky, you can kiss his feet. Darshan.

'You want to do that?'

Dad smiled and said, 'Love is a strange thing, it makes you want to give yourself up. Hand yourself over. You'll do anything.'

What else do I know? That the Knowledge is ancient knowledge. 'Chinese like the I Ching?' I asked.

'No, Indian.' Indian. I said the word aloud. China-India-Vietnam.

Skip skip skip. Faster with my rope, hop hop hop. Kissing feet is gross. Skip. The attic leads to where? Skip here so I can track them. The skin on my palms gets hot from the handles of the skipping rope, and the only way I can cool it down is to blow on my hands.

At bedtime Dad sits on the bed smoking a rollie and asks me what I'm reading.

'*The Family from One End Street.*'

He picks it up and looks at it. 'Cool. Haven't read that one.'

'Okay.'

He stands. 'Night, Sue.'

'Dad, will you tell me the Knowledge?'

He is surprised, blows smoke upwards, shakes his head. 'I pledged to keep it a secret. You know that.'

'Why?'

'Because it's sacred.'

'But I'm good with secrets. Please, Dad, I really want to understand. I think it will be like... protection, at school, you know?' I think of the conversations I've heard with him and Bill. 'I have this thirsty feeling, Dad.'

He looks at me, interested now. 'What do you mean, thirsty?'

I sit up in bed. 'Like there must be more to life, more than school and all this.'

He smiles. He rubs his beard. Spiritual Thirst is one of his favourite topics. 'You're a bit young to have thoughts like that.'

'I don't see why. Kids are humans. They feel things too.'

'True,' he says, rubbing his beard. He looks pleased. 'I guess you are quite a special child. You could get it, maybe?' He takes a long minute to think, and then coughs and sits up closer to me on the bed. 'Well, okay, but it is a very, very sacred secret.' He jabs his cigarette out in the pot of a half-dead cactus on the mantelpiece.

'I understand.' I sit up. Focused.

'The first one, the most important one, is the light. Divine Light.' He makes me face him as he speaks. His eyes are shiny, and his face is a bit twitchy.

'Okay.'

'Some people spend years, decades even, figuring out how to meditate. They go and live in a cave. Under a tree. But the thing about this is...'

'Yes?'

'It's exciting. And it happens fast.'

'What does?'

'Okay, I'll try to show you. Put your fingertips on your eyelids,' he says, and he shows me. 'You do this.' He puts his thumb and middle finger near his eye and strokes across each closed eyelid, starting at the corner of the eye and working out.

I copy him, press my fingers on my eyelids.

'Do you see colours, swirls?'

'Am I supposed to press hard?'

'No, not hard, but with some pressure, you're supposed to feel it.'

I push my fingertips along the skin as he showed me.

'Do you see it? Lights?'

'Ummm… I think so.' There are light swirls, but it's the same as I normally get, going to bed or if I have a headache.

Dad's voice gets louder. 'Do you see it, Sue?' He claps his hands.

I open my eyes and blink. He looks excited, but also guilty. I try again. I don't know. 'Yeah…'

'That's just a taste,' he says, like as if he's given me Turkish delight – like the Queen of Narnia – or the best chocolate in the world. 'A thousand suns, it's called, and it's spiritual.'

'Okay,' I say, trying to think. Was it spiritual? Does that mean I will float? Or dissolve?

'It's like a light show, and if you keep doing it with absolute faith, with love, from the heart, from the solar plexus, then you will eventually see him, the Guru, the Lord of the Universe, inside that light, and it will be imprinted on your eyeballs, and in your soul.'

I frown. Is the solar plexus in the sky? 'Do you see it, Dad, when you do it?' I ask.

'Yeah, sometimes, rarely, but you have to feel it. It has to be the right feeling, and you have to be open to it. With the techniques, it's exciting – like a show. Fireworks.'

I press again. I want so much to see the fireworks in my eyes. 'I think I see it,' I say, unsure.

He hugs me, sort of jittery all over. 'I'm not supposed to... really not supposed to divulge, so you've got to swear to keep it a secret, okay?'

Keep the pressing on my eyeballs a secret? 'Why?'

'Because it's one of the ancient techniques. From the Himalayas. From Tibet.'

'Tell me the next one?'

He shakes his head. 'I can't, I can't,' he says, looking worried now. 'You won't tell Bill? Or Mum? That I told you?'

'No, Dad, don't worry.'

'It'll be our...'

'Secret.' I finish the sentence for him. I'm better than he knows at secrets. I pat his hand to reassure him.

'Are you sure you saw it?' he asks me again, head tipped on the side as he's at the door. 'You might not have done. It's to do with the mind. The light show inside you. Powerful, right? Beautiful, devised by Him. It gives you power. It's perfect.'

'Is there science behind it?' I say.

He laughs, comes back towards me, and ruffles my hair. He grins. 'Little questioner, little thinker,' he says. 'You're right to ask it, but the scientists don't know. They'll just say we need to test this. They won't understand that it's a feeling. That it comes out of experience and belief, not fact.'

'Thanks, Dad,' I say, and he hugs me again, the stubble beard, the strong whiff of Golden Virginia.

'I know it doesn't make much sense now, but what I've told you... but what I've given you is pure nectar. Truth.'

'Right.'

He starts coughing, intense enough to make his whole body shudder. When he is done, he says 'Shh', as if I am the one making all the noise.

I listen to the satsang noise in bed, telling myself it all makes sense now. I focus on the Y-crack on the ceiling.

School is the illusion, it is meaningless, nothing; at home, the walk to the Sanctuary is real. Fingers on the eyelids, press lightly, see the lights? I've finally got the first step in. I won't be left behind.

Later in the week, I ask him to play the tapes in my room as I go to sleep, and he is pleased. He sets up the cassette player for me in the corner. Finally, I'm allowed into their garden, into their places. The voice comes in, over and over, every night, through the pillow and the air. There's one bit I like. I play it again and again. Rewind play rewind play.

The point of perfection is all lighted up and waiting for us.

We go in there, peek our heads in there, and see it.

It's just light and light and light and light and light and light and light.

'It's my birthday on Thursday,' Mandy Brown says, hair a-frizz, bluish circles under her eyes, making her finger and thumb into a circle as if about to spy through it. I count chewing gum spots on the playground. Seven. 'Something you want to say?'

I glance around. I'm looking for Gemma to see if she's there; she might help me. The tide of uniformed kids coming into school parts around us, nobody looking, no sign of Gemma. 'Happy birthday,' I say in a robotic voice. The drizzle makes it through the seams of my coat.

'I'd like a present. If you can afford one. Or are you too poor? Because my mum thinks you have no money and you get all your food out of the skip behind the Co-op, is that the case?'

I shake my head.

'I'm having a birthday tea,' she says. 'If you want to drop round with a card with some money then we'll know you don't eat out of the bins, won't we? Or are you too poor?'

I walk away.

'Your family is so poor they eat out of bins,' she shouts at my back.

Out of context. What? But I don't reply.

By the time I reach the doors to the school, I've counted eighty-seven chewing gum spots. I walk into an English class. When I sit down, the person near me gets up and moves. The next class is the same. In maths, I sit next to Nikki, usually shunted due to her weird name and old parents, but even she moves away from me.

At lunchtime, I manage to find Gemma near the science block door, and she explains. Mandy Brown has let it be known that I am not to be spoken to on account of a run-in between my mum, who had for the first time in years gone to a hairdresser, and Mandy's mum, who happened to work there as a hair-washer. Mum asked her to turn down the temperature of the water. Mandy Brown's mum actively increased the heat and eventually told my mum she was a dirty, disgusting, commie freak, and my mum went crazy in front of women having their hair permed.

'But why am I getting it? I'm not my mum.'

Gemma scuffs the concrete with her feet. 'I don't know. She's just really mean,' she says, and moves away with sorry eyes.

At home, in the living room, we are watching *Blankety Blank*, the quiz show where the prize is a cheque to be filled in.

I bring up what happened at school today. 'No one will talk to me because of you, Mum,' I say.

'Oh, that woman is awful.' She is knitting a long, mis-shapen blue jumper. 'She's a real bitch. She commented on my shoes, my hair, my nose.'

'But what did you do, Mum? You went crazy?' I looked at her. She was a bit sheepish, a bit avoiding my eye.

'I shouted. I threw a cup of tea at her.'

'Oh my God.'

'Don't worry, Sue,' Dad says. 'The conveyor belt of school and work is just a temporary illusion...'

Blankety Blank Blankety Blank.

'It's not though, is it?' I say. 'It's school. It's real.' In bed my fingers are hot. Down in the bottom of my head I know

I won't be able to sleep until I've written it all out, so I write the words I associate with school. A catalogue of my reality. *Playground. Teacher. Desk. Chewing gum. Alone. Canteen. Walking there. Crisps. Toilets. Shouting. Alone. Alone. Alone.* Then I write the words I associate with my parents' world. *Mind. Breath. Ego. Focus/Mirror. Thirst. Life purpose. Peace. Happiness. Path. Self. Heart. Knowledge.* Stupid. My fingers hurt. The words on my parents' list look nicer than the school ones. I squint and rub my eyes. They ache, they blur.

Then I write *Freak. Weird. Hippy. Red. Commie.*

The living room is empty when I get home from school the next day. On the mantelpiece is an envelope with the money for the milkman. £3.50. I take it, grab my bike and cycle to Mandy's house. It's a council house, but slightly bigger than ours because it's on a corner. From the gate, I can see the shifting shadows of a party going on inside. I hear the song 'Relax' playing. Mandy answers the door wearing deely-boppers and glitter stars on her cheeks. Behind her, most of our classmates are shifting around, holding carton drinks with straws. I sway on the step, for some reason thinking of wild dogs and what they must do for food. How it must feel, out in the fields with nowhere to get in and warm at night.

'Yes?'

I hold out the money in my palm. 'I don't have a card, but here's the money for something.'

She looks at the £3.50 in my hand, takes it and puts it in a dish near the door full of coins and cash. 'Thanks,' she says and kicks a balloon out of the way of her feet before shutting the door.

I'm reading in my room when Mum comes in, trailing wool, holding her needles in one hand.

'Sue, have you seen the milk money? I have to put it out for the morning.'

I don't look up from my book. There's a long pause, a prickle on my palm.

'Sue, have you seen the envelope that was on the mantelpiece?'

She comes up close and waits. I can feel a fury, moveable anger that is never far away from her. After a long silence, she bends, snatches the book out of my hand and throws it on the bed. I won't look up.

'Are you kidding me? You took it? Don't you realize that we have no other money?' Eyes on my bed, on the skin on my wrist.

She turns around and looks at all my books. I spend a long time arranging them. Sometimes I put them in alphabetical order. Currently they are by the colour of the spine. She casts her arm in a big bow, aiming for a dramatic gesture.

'What if I sell all of these? Take them away?'

I pull my knees up towards myself.

'Dave needs milk to sleep, you know that.' She disappears downstairs.

I hear loud voices and then Dad appears. 'What's going on? Why did you take the milk money?'

'I had to give it to Mandy Brown as birthday money.'

Mum is behind him, hovering. 'What? This is getting worse. You give our milk money to that woman? That woman who was so cruel, so horrible, so vicious to me? Why would you give her our money? Our milk money?'

Dad frowns. 'Stand up, Sue. Why?'

I stand up next to the bed, staring at the floor like some kind of thief in a shop caught with all the sweets in my pocket, the virulent skin-crawl of disappointed parents. The tangle of kid life… impossible to explain. I think about a history lesson we'd had recently about communists, the slogans, civic notices, the drawings of hammers and stars. 'It was her birthday.'

They both shout at me now, their words falling around me as if someone is throwing plates or cups. Crashing. Banging. No money. Money is tight. Milk important. What was I thinking? Who cares that it's Mandy Bloody Brown's birthday? Stealing money is very bad.

Then Dad, even more furious than Mum now, grabs my coat and makes me put it on, squeezing my wrist hard. 'Go and get the money back, right now,' he says.

'I can't, Dad, that's so embarrassing. Honestly, I can't do that.'

'You can. Now.' They are together, resolute, my mum's lips tight and severe, Dad's eyes sharp on me. He stands up straight. 'Shit, I've got to go now,' he says. He's off for a night shift. 'Go and get the money and bring it back and give it to your mum so your little brother can have milk at bedtime, okay?' His face is white and deadly.

I slope out of the front door. Once our road seemed enormous, but now it is closing, shrinking, and I can't get the
strength up to button my coat. *Your family is so poor they eat
out of bins...* I look at a woman pulling her cardigan tight
around herself at the bus stop. Isn't everyone poor around
here? Doesn't almost everyone sign on? The queue for the
dole money at the post office is always long. Catalogues.
Hire purchase. Provvy woman. I kick a crisp packet along
the kerb until it flurries away from me.

Mandy's mum answers this time, scowling-faced in a
dressing gown, and calls for Mandy.

'I need the money back,' I say, cheeks burning, staring at
the floor. 'It was for the milkman.'

Mandy smirks, scrabbles around in her bowl of coins and
gives me £3. I don't ask for the fifty pence.

As I walk away, she shouts, 'Commie, hippy, weirdo
scum.'

I press RECORD.

Speak into the microphone. Experiment: talk in your
secrets, breathe them. Record. Better to capture words on
the sticky brown audio tape than type black marks on to
the white page. It's safer. I put my cassette collection into
my Museum suitcase and keep it under my bed. I begin a
catalogue of recordings: *Sue. Morning, June. 1985.* I tape
Dave (boring). Dad's shaving noises.

'Sue, that's bloody creepy, can you stop it!' Mum is in the
kitchen, frowning at a bowl of mung bean shoots. Disgusting;
they look like little commas.

'Why have you stopped talking, Mum? You never stop talking, why now?'

She looks at the tape player, suspicious. 'Turn it off,' she says. 'Take it away.'

I try Nana. 'Speak into it, Nana,' I say, pressing RECORD again.

It sends her into a reverie. 'Uncle Stanley has to check his room every time he gets off a shift for microphones and bugs put there by the Stasi. God knows why.' She stares off out of the window at private memories, then turns to me. 'Get away with you now, nobody wants to hear me a-rabbiting or any of that monkey business, get aways.'

Kaleidoscope

It was the ward sister who called me.

'It's a bang to the head, but I've checked it and cleaned the wound, which is slight. She was apparently down on the sea's edge. It was around midnight.'

The coast road was clear at that time, and when I got to Mum's flat the ward sister, whose name I couldn't remember, let me in. She told me they'd been at a consultant's retirement party in a pub near the hospital earlier that evening. Mum was asleep, with a small bandage taped to her forehead. She had a scrape on her nose too. She was curled on her side, and there was a fading smell of alcohol in the room.

'Suzanne,' she said. 'Haven't seen you for years. You look well.' The ward sister was a bit younger than Mum. In her early sixties perhaps. She looked tired and immediately patted her pockets for keys and looked around for her bag.

'Do I need to stay up?'

'No, just near her. For one night. Keep an eye on her. She'll be okay, but…' She rubbed her cheek. 'She seemed very unstable.' She gave me a look.

'You think she was trying to...' Mum hated the sea in winter, said it made her feel heavy and oppressed. Since developing all her lung problems, she was afraid of the winter months, the wind, howl and dampness. It made her retreat and hide from the world, and it sucked her inside. She'd once said to me, 'I smoked because I was sad, and now I am sad because I am forced inside because I smoked.'

'I'm sorry,' the ward sister said. 'I should have stopped her drinking earlier. She got into an argument with one of the nurses and stormed off. Luckily one of the groups followed her down there and saw her slip on the edge of the groyne. Honestly, I don't know what she was planning to do. It was probably all instinct. And booze. Tell her she needs to come in tomorrow, and we'll have another look and check her head. I'm not on duty, thank God – the state of me.' She laughed. 'But I've left a message.'

The large windows of Mum's flat did not leave much room for privacy. I sat down on the chair opposite her bed and closed my eyes. My fingers twitched. I was wired. I texted my husband and told him I was going to stay over. I hadn't slept in the same room as my mum for decades. I went to the loo and put the kettle on.

I doodled houses, waiting to see if she would wake up. It was the first time I had drawn in a long time, and as I did it opened up space for old phrases. Instead of blocking them as I usually do, this time I let them in. *Pitched roof. Rafters.* Instructions filtered into my head from pages read long ago. *Owner-built homes. Spaceship Earth. Dome roof. Ventilation. Hot air in and downward and out. Composting.*

Mum would be mortified in the morning. She was retired now, but the hospital colleagues and what they thought of her meant a lot. There was a sound from the street. A gaggle of drunk people walking past, and a bin being kicked. Then quiet again.

Could I pinpoint exactly when things went wrong? I remembered getting a call in my first year at university. I had worked my way through the UCAS book in the library on my own and figured out the loan stuff. A call came in, Mum's voice. 'Sue, come home, I'm leaving Dad, you have to get your stuff.' It was the second term of the first year. I got the National Express to London and then down to Eastbourne. A long, sluggish journey, and I'd brought the wrong books – Phenomenology, too difficult – and I felt sorry for myself as I put my cheek on the glass window and looked out at the rainy sky.

Dad answered the door, looking like a skeleton. 'I didn't think you were coming until tomorrow,' he said, letting me in. The house stank of cigarettes, coffee.

'Where's Mum?' I asked.

'Gone for a walk.'

That was weird. She never did that.

'Wasn't anyone going to tell me this was happening? What's going on, Dad?' We went into the kitchen and my dad put the kettle on. He looked reduced, as if the core of him had been zapped out, lasered.

'Mum said she wrote, explained to you?'

I'd never got a letter. Just the weird phone call in the night where I'd stood near the communal phone in my student halls. I'd been in bed with a gentle, sweet, acne-pockmark-faced boy.

'I'm leaving Dad.'

Parents splitting up was a ten-a-penny occurrence. Parents splitting up was so normal that you were the odd one out if your parents hadn't separated, yet still it was as if something deep down in me was coming up to the surface, summoned.

'I'm sorry, Dad,' I said. He had his elbow on the kitchen table. A cat they'd recently got and named Sophie slithered around his leg. It was too intelligent and seemed possessive of my dad. I didn't much like it. Dad looked lost, sad, old and broken. I wondered why they'd got a new cat at a time like this.

Dave poked his head in. It was clear he had discovered smoking weed, and the smell of it wafted into the room. When Dad was in the loo he said, 'It's been grim. Lots of fighting.' He disappeared upstairs, obviously not wanting to go into anything, and turned up Rage Against the Machine.

Dad didn't return from the loo. I was left alone in this kitchen that didn't feel too clean. Everything had a sticky, oily surface, as if bacon had been cooked in it for years, and yet I didn't think either of them ate bacon. But who knew, now, what anyone did or believed in any more? Nobody wanted to talk to me. Here I was in this small kitchen, for nothing. On the floor under the table, I noticed some boxes; Mum was beginning an old-style purge.

I went up to my bedroom. I swung open the doors to my built-in wardrobe and saw that the clothes I hadn't taken with me were bagged up in bin liners. Only a few things remained on hangers. I heard the front door slam and reluctant steps on the stairs. She put her head around the door with no explanation of where she'd been and no reference to the fact that I'd just trekked back from uni. Her right eye twitched and she couldn't look at me. She looked older than just a few weeks ago, when I'd waved goodbye. 'Hello,' she said, coming in and sitting on the bed.

'Everything's going so fast,' I said.

She seemed stripped down and weak. I had wanted to shout at her, but now we were in my small bedroom together that impulse faded. She was the catalyst, from what I could tell, of the final annihilation of what was already a loosely, barely held together family unit.

'God, Mum,' I said, 'what's happening to your skin?' She'd had a flare-up of psoriasis – her and Dave's joint fate – and her nose and forehead were covered in sore, dry patches and scabs.

'Stress-related,' she said, and I noticed her hands were shaking.

'Dad said you wrote me a letter, but I never got it.'

She looked genuinely surprised. 'You didn't? I sent it. Last week. Telling you that... I'm leaving Dad.'

'Yeah, well, I know that now. Why?' It was exactly the wrong moment, but for some reason I remembered the smell of being in bed with a boy and how simple and easy that place was and wished very much that I was back there.

'It's complicated. That's why I wrote it all down.'

'Maybe you can rewrite it?'

She shook her head.

'Can't you remember what you wrote? Can't you just tell me now?' She wiped her eye. Either it was watering or she was beginning to cry. I looked at her skin. She looked terrible. Separating, I could see, was terrible. She then began to full-on cry.

'I didn't know how to tell you. I kept waiting and waiting. I thought I would sort out the practical stuff first. I wrote to the council to tell them that I was leaving, and they wrote back and said that because Dave has turned eighteen and you have left home then we no longer "constitute a family".'

I sat down on the chair next to my old desk. It was covered in stickers and Post-it notes with smiley faces. I had a violent wish to get drunk, quickly.

'Why did you go and tell them that?'

'Well, I had to tell them because I'm moving out. So then I went in to explain and said, "I'm moving out, but not them. They are still a family," and they said, "They are not, and they are being evicted."' She looked desolate, staring at the floor.

My chair creaked as I swivelled slightly on it. 'I don't understand what that means, Mum. Where will we live?'

'That's the thing,' she said. 'Dad and Dave will now have to find somewhere to live, a flat to rent, and I will get my own.'

I looked at her. 'What about me?'

'Well, you live in the university halls, don't you?'

I looked at my hands. 'Only in term time, Mum.'

Then she said, 'I'm stopping the Maharaj Ji stuff. Your dad wants to carry on. I'm forty-one. I still have some years, time. Dad's very, very difficult to be with.'

'Have you got another bloke?' I said.

She shook her head. 'No.'

I got up from the chair and moved away from her, towards the window. I glanced at the door; could I get a National Express coach out of here? It was not going to be possible to sleep in here tonight. I would suffocate. I would explode. I would disintegrate.

'Sue, has your student loan come in?'

'Yes,' I said. My eyes were dry. The house was different. It had shrunk and contorted. Was the size of the rooms of the house directly in correlation to the fact that I'd been having sex, so far my main educational development at uni? Was each new roll in the sack an inch off the corner diameter of the childhood room? Only this wasn't my childhood room or house, I didn't have one, and why was I thinking about sex anyway? Everything about this visit home was depressing. And then I fully registered what she was saying. 'Why, do you need money?' I said.

She nodded then, and all the words flooded out. I can't do it any more, be with him, take it, too much, too difficult... never any money. Giving it away. Crushing. Can't do it any more. Depression. Black moods. No money. Maharaj Ji. Need space. Need own room. Own Life. I'm not that old. I must live my life. I need this. I need more.

'How much do you need?' I said, to stop it all, though what I felt right then was hate. I was due to get £4,000 for the year. I would need to supplement it with a bar job or something. I didn't have to pay fees, but it wasn't enough. It came in instalments. I'd just had £1,200 for this term.

She coughed and climbed off the bed and stood bolt upright. 'Eight hundred and fifty pounds for a deposit for a flat. Plus. A little bit more as I have to pay some bills.' There was an odd dignity to the way she asked me this.

I realized that she had a movie playing in her head around emancipation and fresh beginnings. The possibility of a life outside of marriage to a difficult, depressive man whom she had been with since her teens. A flat. Room of her own. A window. A lover. A different, less exhausting way of being that doesn't involve serving children's whims and needs. I guessed she'd waited; I'd heard this line on the TV: let's wait till the kids have gone to university and then break up the family – and then, freedom. She had dreamed it all and plotted and not thought about small realities like council houses that you are only eligible to live in if you are a family.

'I'll give you the money, Mum,' I said, and her shoulders dropped, in relief, in emotional exhaustion. I saw a tiny glint of desperation, but then she hid it quickly. 'I'm going back,' I said. 'Don't think I can sleep here.'

'Go tomorrow. Also, you've got to take whatever you want to keep. I need to clear it all out.' She did a sweeping motion with her hand, spreading this way and that. It was quite a flourish. Kali Yuga purge.

I sat in my room. It was full of everything I'd accumulated since moving to Eastbourne, when I'd got old enough to stop her from throwing things away without my permission. I picked up an old pencil case. I looked through some drawers. I didn't know where to begin with salvaging stuff.

Worries percolated at the perimeter of my brain: Where to stay outside of term times? Where to keep my stuff? How to live if I give Mum all my student loan?

As I sifted through my old jumpers and t-shirts, I thought what a selfish person it was who left a husband and kids and made everyone fall apart and end up homeless. But this didn't chime with the reading I'd been doing all term. Kate Millett. Adrienne Rich. Toni Morrison. A whole generation of women writers whose work I was starting to love, all of whom had left their husbands, looking for some form of freedom beyond these square houses.

In some ways, I finally had what I was looking for. It was the release of the tension that had always been there. I'd had a *Wizard of Oz* poster on the wall when I was little, and it used to frighten me. It was the scene of the cyclone, of the house spinning and flying and coming-to to a new reality. I always felt that our house and home would be destroyed and that Mum would destroy it. I always knew it was coming, and maybe now I could breathe, because everything I'd been dreading was happening.

I'm homeless, I said to myself. It was floaty, weird, new, scary, electric.

She turned in her bed and the central heating system of the whole building – Soviet-style, coming on without warning in October and not to be turned off until spring – made a grumbling noise. She coughed a bit and then pulled herself up and blinked at me. 'Sue? What are you doing here?' She rubbed her eyes, looked exhausted, hangover coming in.

'The ward sister called me. She was nice. I don't know how she had my number.' I looked down at the floor. 'Are you going back to sleep? Do you want me to stay or go? They want to have another look at your head tomorrow.'

She put her hand on the bandage. 'Who did this? Lizzie?' That was her name, I remembered now.

'Yes.'

She closed her eyes again, then another big coughing fit closed them again.

'Go back to sleep, Mum, it's okay.'

She made a groaning noise and slunk down into the bed.

Time moved slowly as she slept her unhappy sleep. I drew houses from stories heard a long time ago. I was drawing them for clues. Why do you go to the sea? Why do you want to leave us? I drew blueprints of houses. Squares and spaces. A back bent over the stew, the pulling up of a weed in the flower bed. There was a running joke in the family that my nana looked like Florrie from the cartoon strip *Andy Capp*. And my Grandad Paddy looked like Andy, hero of northern working-class life. Florrie on the doorstep with a black eye, saying to her friend, *I was talkin' when I should've been listenin'*. And another one of the captions: *Look here, honey, I'm a man of few pleasures, an' one of them 'appens to be knocking yer about*. The flinch in the eye when Nana asks Grandad Paddy for rent money. This is handbag-housekeeping. The cash in the envelope, hiding it from the husband. And all through those years social housing tenancies were always signed in the husband's name.

I drew and drew, circle to square as Mum slept. In my mind and drawings, a story:

The man in the council offices smokes at his desk (it is still the time of smoking in offices). *You say you cannot stay in a house with your husband, Paddy, for one moment more because he pisses the rent money on the racing and in the Butcher's Arms. Oh, and he takes to his Andy Capp role too well.* The man behind the desk says, *I know Paddy, he's a Butcher's regular.* He laughs.

He goes on. *I know the one about Paddy playing the Irish bagpipes on the front line and being shot in the arse, shrapnel in his bottom, saving his life and getting him out of the worst of the fighting.* He stops laughing and says, *If you leave, Mrs McGee, then the tenancy is over. Family only in those tenancies, and what is a family without a mother?*

I drew more houses: my dad, born in a maternity hospital – square windows, triangle roofs, scary basements, big, cold kitchens – to my Welsh nana, who was unmarried, undecided on whether to give him up or not, until finally my grandad was sent home from the army and forced to marry her, and then he never stopped punishing them all. I thought of my Welsh nana's words: If I leave him, my husband, who's been beating the children for years, and this is the eighties by now and I am tired, my body is tired, breasts hanging and folds of skin between the thighs and an endless cycle of thrush and infection and leakage and despair, do I have access to his Rolls-Royce money?

Ah, the solicitor says, *no.*

But what I didn't know, and what I was drawing to find, was how to help my mum with all this behind her. Behind us.

With the crack, and the swig, the whisky and the shouting, how could you get away? You could step out, with your hair long, and look eastwards to where they meditate, to soft, golden voices giving you other ways. When a funny man crouches, offers you a joint, tells you of places such as the Naropa School of Disembodied Poetics or the Prem Nagar Ashram in Haridwar, and speaks of transpersonal transubstantiation, you might nod, and go up the narrow stairs with him, but why does this mean you want to go into the sea tonight?

I put down the pen and stood up. I had to get out of there.

Lattice floaters crystal haloes drifted patterns in my vision. It happened sometimes when I flew or when I was tired, but today they seemed to have a distinct organization to them, like a grid.

I remembered going on holiday to a caravan park in Caernarfon, back in the day. A week of rain. Allowed one thing each from the shop. I chose a kaleidoscope and obsessively moved around the caravan looking at things through it.

'Why do you like it so much?' Mum said. I was pointing the kaleidoscope at a full ashtray.

'It makes everything beautiful,' I said, looking at the rollies and piles of ash fragmented into ever-repeating triangles.

She took it off me and looked through it. 'Oh yeah,' she said. 'It does. I can see it.'

I left before she woke. About 6.45 in the morning. I made sure the door was closed firmly and quietly and didn't leave a note.

Detached House, Early 1980s

They are in a flap because they think I've eaten the acid. They call it a tab. They hold my face, peer into my eyes, someone is crying at the top of the stairs. 'Is she tripping?' I say nothing, looking at a wasp drowning in a glass of orange juice.

Bill tells a story about being hauled into school because of his daughter's behaviour. 'They said if we aren't careful that she might end up... smoking.' Bill and my dad light their rollie cigarettes, giggling.

'I'll make tea,' Carys says. We are at a table on a veranda made from old railway sleepers. She looks at me. 'Want to help?' I scramble up to follow her.

Bill and Carys's house stands on its own in the middle of a twisting country lane in Shropshire. As well as being a leading Premie, Bill is a piano tuner, which seems like a fairy-tale job to me, up there with elf shoemaker and beanstalk grower. His workshop is full of the skeletons and teeth of broken-up pianos and the corrugated roof is covered in passion-flower vines. There is even an orchard in their garden with apple, plum and pear trees.

There are two little boys, two older brothers and an older girl, Harmony. She is the only one I'm interested in. She wears army-issue jackets over tiny cut-off jeans and Doc Martens. Her new breasts show through her t-shirt, and I know from earwigging that she's lived in ashrams, the ones where babies are shared and no one is called Mum. Maharaj Ji's voice drones through the open kitchen window: *Satguru has come, freedom, freedom, all mankind is gonna be as one, love is all, all is one...* Dave is playing 'Anarchists' and 'Kill Thatcher!' We are here because Bill has been teaching Dad how to drive and later there's going to be a big satsang. Mum isn't here yet, she's working, but she will be picked up later.

Carys never sits down. She floats and moves things around. Small kids run up to her and cry or climb on her for a second and then run off again.

The whole family apart from Bill have thick black hair. Carys's has an impressive stripe of grey at the front and her dress is a complicated flowery fabric. Their house is the first I've ever been to that is like the houses in books I love. Edwardian. Kitchen garden. Secret door. Ghosts of wise gardeners. Yellow wallpaper that will survive wars and weather. Their kitchen is a mess but nice. I run my fingers over large, red-coloured tiles on the wall and admire the depth of the enormous white sink. I press my hand on the big oak table. It is so different from our house, or Gemma's. There's a picture of Harmony Blue-Tacked to the wall. Her tongue is sticking out and she has a nasal spray stuck in her nose. I put my head on the table, like a kid in a boring maths lesson, and watch her fill the kettle. 'Is my mum coming later?' I ask.

'Think so. Not sure who's going to drive and get her with the state of those two, though.' She points out of the window.

I tune in to the cassette. *My world lights up I want you to know. I love you Maharaj Ji, Oh Maharaj Ji I really love you Maharaj Ji, oh! Look inside your heart, and see if you do have a missing link. I have got this Truth, and I am revealing this Truth to people because I know, and I have experienced it. And more than a million people have experienced it with me. But first, I want you to find out for yourself, do you need it, do you want it, are you ready for it?*

'Want some ice cream?' Carys says, with a touch on my shoulder. I nod. She hands me a pink bowl. 'You don't want to listen?' She gestures to the cassette player. I hadn't realized, but I'd put my hands over my ears. I don't know what to say.

If you are, and if you want it, you are more than welcome to receive it if you understand I am not a liar... She walks over and stops his voice.

'Don't worry. I get it. Sometimes I don't want to listen either. Go into the pantry and choose whatever flavour you want from the freezer.'

The freezer is huge. We don't have one. I heave it open and look at enough food to last a century. There is a box of apples from the orchard on the floor next to it. I pick one up, crunch into it and immediately feel a tooth shift. It's been loose for a week or so now. Bill's voice comes through the kitchen, and I peek through the gap in the pantry door with the apple in my mouth.

Carys says, 'Bill, lay off the psychedelics tonight with the kids all here.' Bill says something in a low voice. I can't hear it. Carys's face is covered by straggly orange hair. He leans in close. She has her back to the sink.

'You can't disguise it a bit?' he says.

'What?' Carys has a different face than the one she uses with me.

'You know what.'

'I can't hide it because I don't want to. I asked you not to do it with the kids here.'

When he is gone, I watch her. She stares down at the flint tiles on the kitchen floor and puts her palm on her forehead as if to stop herself from falling forwards.

I pull the apple out of my mouth. My tooth is wedged in the white bit and there is a dot of blood. Harmony is in the kitchen now. Carys says, 'Where have you been?'

'Nowhere,' Harmony says, moving fast through the room, slamming a door.

I put the tooth on the shelf to get later, pick up a jar of fermented watermelon rind and hold it in both hands. I count to five hundred before I move.

The kitchen is empty. There is a little ashtray the shape of a whale on the windowsill, his snout one end, his tail the other. In it, one sheet of paper with lines drawn on it like a grid. And another, where the squares have been cut out neatly. Origami. Or confetti. I am arranging them on the windowsill, then Bill comes back in.

'Sue. Sue. Have you put one of those in your mouth?' I hear him chuckling to himself.

*

I wander down the garden path. Harmony is lurking behind a tree, and I sidle towards her. She points to what looks like a den. 'Want to come in?'

It's a half-collapsed geodesic dome built in the corner of their field. I follow her through the entrance. Inside, it smells of wet dog. We sit cross-legged opposite each other and listen to the rain. The pattering on the dome is nice.

'Where do you stand on the Guru?' She pokes her blue fingernails under the strip of black lace on her neck. 'For, or against?' It's weird to be around kids who speak the same language.

'About Maharaj Ji?'

'Yeah.'

'Not sure,' I say.

She pulls out a packet of Cutters Choice tobacco and some cigarette papers and begins to roll. I watch her pink tongue lick the paper. 'Our dad,' she says, 'waves an amethyst up and down our bodies after school to get rid of the bad energy from the "English state education system".'

I laugh.

'He's so embarrassing. I make him wait for us around the corner so nobody sees him.' She uncrosses her legs, and then her face shifts as the weather does. She puts her rolled cigarette in her mouth and lies on her stomach, bending her legs up in the air behind her. Stares at me. 'So, do you believe?'

I focus on a constellation of freckles on my arm. 'In what?'

'In the Guru?'

'Not sure,' I say again, worried I sound thick and pointless. 'But yes, I think so.' She smiles, and I have no idea what it means. I want to seem older than I am. Wiser, cooler. 'I meditate,' I say. 'I'm allowed to do it.' I watch as she narrows her eyes.

'You do?'

I am casual; it's nothing, yeah, as my dad says, I'm down with it all. 'Sure.'

'Don't you find it totally boring?' She stands up and rummages around in one of the many piles of junk behind her. She pulls out a stick. I recognize it; my dad has one.

'What's that?'

'Don't they call it a beragon or something?' She puts the T-shaped stick in front of her and rests her chin on it. 'To meditate the whole day through.' She laughs and sticks her tongue up, then stands, letting the beragon fall. I can see she's had enough of me.

She wipes her body as if getting rid of invisible grass and offers me a cigarette. 'Want?'

I shake my head.

'Okay. See ya later, you can stay in here if you like.'

When she's gone, I lie back on the floor of the geodome. Posters are pasted all over the ceiling. There are cut-outs and printouts from the Vietnam War. Vietnam! Peace not war! NO TO THE BLOODY WAR. STOP THE SLAUGHTER. Across the entire roof of the geodome, it's like being on the inside of a papier-mâché balloon. Vietnamese faces. Signs. Peace. People. Love. I lick my lips, but I can't stop the dryness. Then I can't sit still. Vietnam. India. China. How can I get there? I must get there.

In the corner of the dome is an old wardrobe with no handles on the door. I tug it open and inside there are shelves of board games. All the usual. Scrabble. Monopoly. I pull out a jigsaw puzzle. It has a picture of a bird's feather, magpie, I think. I tip the pieces out on to the floor and flip them out on the filthy carpet so they are all right side up.

'We're watching *Ghostbusters* tonight,' someone calls.

I start trying to fix the puzzle together, beginning with the corners. But behind the feather are individual strands of grass and leaves. So much green. The feather itself is impossible. It would take me forever; I don't even know where to begin.

I shift in my sleeping bag and curl my knees up to my chest.

'Harmony,' I whisper, looking over towards her sleeping bag. I want to tell her that I hate attics, but she is asleep and looks peaceful. All the kids have been put in what they call the 'playroom' so that the adults can use the bedrooms. Mum has been picked up after work and is downstairs. Carys has left.

I creep out of my sleeping bag and go downstairs to retrieve my tooth. I know no tooth fairy is coming anywhere near this attic in Shropshire, but I want it anyway. I move as quietly as I can. I sneak past the living room door and look through the gap.

It is quite dark in the room, just two lamps on and some lit candles. Nag champa burning, of course.

Surprisingly, it is my mum talking. 'I'm not so sure,' she says.

'You'll get there.' Bill says. Mum is on the floor in front of him, he's behind her on the sofa with his hands on her shoulders. The air is thick with smoke.

Dad is also on the sofa, but with his eyes closed. There are other people there I recognize from the gatherings at our house. A woman I don't know crawls across the floor until she is in front of the fireplace, where a giant picture of Maharaj Ji is leaning. She bends her head down, puts her forehead on the carpet and her bum in the air. Stays there.

Bill's hands massage my mum's shoulders. I reverse back into the blackness of the hall, but I can't get away from his words. 'Humanity!' he shouts. 'This world as we know it is destroying itself. The intellectuals of the world think they know, but they understand nothing. They have finite brains. What's the use of that? They can't know it in the brain. It needs to be experienced to be understood, right? People who understand it, in their hearts, can dig it and feel it, but those who haven't: forget it! Just a dash dash dash and a big question mark. This world they are living in is just illusion, shadow, nothing.'

I walk faster, through the kitchen, to the back door. I shiver, crouch and put my hand on the damp night grass. It is too dark to go into Harmony's geodome without a torch. I try to tune out the noises behind me and think I've achieved it, but the adults have just stopped talking. I wish Gemma were here with her matches. A little fire in the pantry beneath the fermented courgettes. The framed picture of the Guru turning into black dust in a fire. All the Knowledge-seekers running out, crying into the night, their turn to cough and deal with smoke in their lungs. Cough cough cough. Their turn.

Mum comes into the kitchen then. 'You okay, Sue? What are you doing down here?'

Bill materializes behind her. Looks at me and goes to the counter, where he picks a half-smoked joint out of an ashtray and lights it on a gas ring. He sucks on it then holds it towards me. 'Want some? Help bring you down?'

'No.'

Mum comes up. 'Bill, no, do you think…?' He shakes his head.

I look at the two of them, eyes too bright, smiling at each other. I could take a photograph of them, but it would come out badly. Negative, no light. I want to call my dad, but he's cross-legged and ommm-ing in the other room. I know it would come out weird. Together they usher me back in through the kitchen, but they can't see me. They are smiling, giggling even, sharing a private joke. I don't get my tooth. I leave it there, a private offering to Maharaj Ji: take my tooth. I don't have anything else to give you. Let me in.

Pencil Case

I'd taken the train down to Eastbourne, where we'd moved after Crewe. Where my dad still lived. I was nervous about meeting with this person whose childhood was linked, like mine, to the Divine Light Mission. Colin Storrs had emailed. *You said you wanted to speak to other children of DLM people. Tony is your boy.* Now it was lined up I wasn't sure what to say. The windows were steamy and a smell of burning bacon filled the cafe.

It had been decades since I'd last been here. Not much had changed. The same broken Wurlitzer jukebox was in the corner. The whole place had the same strong smell of frying chips and they still served hot chocolate in glasses balanced in metal frames.

He brought the rain into Bianchi's, slamming the door against its hinges. I immediately realized I knew him. That I'd once spent the night with him. Or almost.

'Tony?'

'Yes. Suzanne?'

'Yes.'

He had curly hair and a pockmarked, pale face. He was about my age. He nodded at me and gestured as if offering to get me something. I shook my head.

The way Tony rubbed his cheek nervously gave our meeting the feel of a blind date or a drug deal. There was the sense that it could all go wrong, or perfectly right.

'Thanks for coming,' we both said at the same time.

Colin Storrs had told me that Tony was the child of a Premie in Eastbourne. We small-talked for a minute about weather, then I gave some spiel about research and a 'project'. Did he recognize me? I couldn't tell. I got out my notebook and a pencil case I loved. A friend had made it from a vintage kimono. I held on to it, zipping and unzipping it as we spoke. When his hot chocolate came he stared at it for a bit before drinking. The mirrored wall next to us reflected ourselves. Amy Winehouse's 'Rehab' rang through the cafe. I asked him where he lived in Eastbourne.

'A bedsit. I'm unemployed at the moment.'

'Did you live in an ashram?' I asked.

'They called it a "Premie house", I think, not an ashram. In Meads, on the other side of Eastbourne. My mum didn't have any money, and it made more sense to live like that.'

'Right.'

He talked, and I listened. His mum had been sucked into the Divine Light Mission when she was a single mum and he was eighteen months old. A new man came into her life and suddenly she was in satsangs, lighting incense everywhere.

'I'm like my mum,' he said. 'Careers, that sort of thing, are not for me.'

148 · THE MUSEUM OF LOST AND FRAGILE THINGS

'Right.'

'Did you believe in it all?' He took a sip of his chocolate. 'I meditate, daily. Or I try to.'

'You do? The techniques?'

He nodded. 'My mum kept saying to me, Tony, surrender and follow the techniques. If you do that then it will all come together and work, but you can't question. I didn't go to university. I didn't go anywhere. I stayed with my mum in here and I kept working on it. I rejected a "normal" life. I knew I was special, though I didn't get to... meet him properly for the Knowledge. I had no choice. It was like I was always in it.'

He had a silver ring on every one of his fingers. Celtic cross designs, like the tattoos everyone got in the nineties. He fiddled with them. His nails looked as though he bit them. I looked out at the sky: grey, seaside, England. I was surprised that he was still into it all, but I tried not to show it.

'I'm a musician. But it's hard to make a living, as you know, and I was working in a pub and did this and that, then I worked in a betting shop, but they had to let me go.'

He must live close to my dad, I thought, whose bedsit was around the corner. I hadn't told him I was coming to Eastbourne, nor about my current line of enquiries.

'Do you feel like there's an alien inside you?' he said, surprising me.

'What?'

A bus pulled up on the road outside the cafe, blocking out much of the light. He looked directly at me now. Was he the person I was thinking of from all those years ago?

'Something stolen. But also, the thing inside, like you both don't want it but you don't want to get it out?'

'Yes,' I said. I was surprised at the directness, but in another way it was a relief. 'That is exactly how I feel.' He smiled slightly, and then my mouth felt chalky with guilt. I was a past-dredger, a scar-picker, and I was unsure what I was doing it for.

A family came clanging in through the door, a hot-cheeked babbling toddler, baby, grandparents. 'God, the weather, the stinking weather,' one of them broadcast to the room.

Tony pushed a bit of his curly grey hair from the side of his face. 'I still seek liberation from past *sankharas*, you know? The way to the future lives, the past lives, looking for the peace. To obtain the oneness.'

I took a long breath. 'You still practise the techniques?'

'I do.'

'And your mum, is she still a follower?'

'She died last year,' he said.

'I'm sorry,' I said. The cult specialist I'd spoken to, with her northern voice and her glasses, came to my mind. Ultimately, the fragile coherence of a member's personal identity merges with and relies on group affirmation and validation. If they stray too far from the 'Truth', then their right to exist – as part of that group – is withdrawn. Their right to exist at all comes into question.

'Yeah, it was brutal. I'm still dealing with it,' he said.

What I wanted to ask was: do you think it causes suicidal thoughts, suicidal ideation? But how could I say that? Do you remember me, Tony? I thought. I was sure now that it was him, but he was showing no signs of remembering.

Then I remembered: Eastbourne. 1993ish. I've decided, against Dad's advice, to go to university; I'm waitressing in a fish-and-chip shop for a year to save up. I'm eligible for a loan. I'm poring over the UCAS book. Previously, I worked at Deep Pan Pizza but was fired for calling out the shift manager for stealing waitress tips. I am achingly provincial. My reading is Nabokov, Camus, and my listening is the Cure. I wake one morning, oppressed by the banality of life and the confines of my tight body and decide that today, I must lose my virginity. I've been trying for a few weeks over the long deadly summer, but have failed at each attempt.

I orchestrated a full-blown throwing of self at a customer in Deep Pan, who picked up on the vibes and hung around to meet me after my shift. I took a copy of Kafka's *Amerika* to his house and arranged myself on his bed, only to freak out at the wetness of lips and the insistence and boniness of exploratory fingers. I exited with a spurious excuse, leaving my book behind.

Next, the pub is frequented by sixth-formers and just-before-universityers. Sweat, smoke and people going off to India next month.

I am talking to a curly-haired boy who is nineteenish. I vaguely know him as the weed person. Marijuana is no novelty to me, so I am less inclined to experiment, but my peers from more conservative households are thoroughly excited by this new world. What is it that draws me to him? This time of wanting to have sex but being sexually terrified, of being both enclosed in my own body as if in a protective sheath and deeply, achingly available.

He's always there and everyone knows him. The dealer. His name is Tony. He has stayed behind, in the seaside grey and wind. He gets me a drink and rolls a cigarette. We talk about governments, fascists and aliens. I go back to his flat and try to give him my virginity. I want to get rid of it. It's a massive weight and curse, but like other times I fumble and it's a mess. He's very gentlemanly about it. I apologize, he apologizes. Gracious enough, and he makes tea. I look around his bleak bedsit and he gives me a cassette. It's Joni Mitchell's *Blue*. 'Take it,' he says. 'Thank you.'

'Tony,' I say, 'do you think we met, before?' He looks at me, frowns. Swizzles one of his silver rings.

Memory: light blue sheets, smoky room, bamboo blinds. Noisy seagulls outside and the sense of a life path that isn't leading anywhere successful. I pick up his single-lens camera and squint through the viewfinder at the empty room and his back. As I pull my jeans back on and re-clip my bra, the flavour of regret seeps through me, followed by a panicky feeling of needing to get out of there, quick. I suppose talking about Maharaj Ji was not something we would ever have guessed we had in common. Our Guru demons must have frolicked happily for one night.

'Do you know someone called Bill?' It'll be easier to contain, I think, if I can catch a culprit.

Tony was looking at me, but via the mirror. 'Yeah, I know Bill,' he said, and I scan his face. It's so strange to think that this person here, now, knows the wizard who sits in my head.

'I don't suppose you have a number?'

'Sure, at home,' he said. Then, out of nowhere, despite me being an almost stranger, he said, 'Drinking's been a problem,' like it was an aside. 'Dark thoughts.'

'I'm sorry,' I said. 'Do you think it's connected?'

'To what?'

'Maharaj Ji?'

He didn't reply. I wanted to get out of the cafe now, just as I'd wanted to get out of his bedsit years ago. I fleetingly thought a man walking past my window was my dad and a flutter of guilt for not calling him came through me.

'Tony? Did you do LSD ever? As a kid, I mean. I've been looking into it, and I can't find any data, not in the whole world, around the long-term effects of psychedelic behaviour – whether drugs or meditating – on kids. No one has been in a position to explore it.'

He looked at me with wide eyes. I counted the pockmarks in his cheeks. From a long-ago bout of chickenpox, I suppose. Or acne.

'Tony, do you think the Maharaj Ji stuff makes people... suicidal?'

He rubbed his eyes, then I realized he was crying.

'Shit, I'm sorry. I didn't mean to upset you,' I said.

'I'm sorry,' he said. 'It's okay, though perhaps you should go.' He stood up. Then he sat down again. 'My mum did it. Last year.'

I stared at the table. Desolation, a strong instinct of sifting and recoil, regret and self-hatred at sticking my fingers into his wounds. 'I'm so sorry.'

Council House, 1980s

She is going out. She opens her knitted cardigan and shows me a leotard and leggings as proof. 'I'm really going to yoga, you know?'

'Okay.'

'Dave's in bed. Can you go up soon?'

'Yep.' Her right eye closes, and her face turns away from me. I do my rounds of the house when she's gone and pick up some of Dave's Lego. I stand near the phone for a second to see if it will ring. It doesn't. I get myself a drink of water and go to bed. Cross-legged, I look at the picture of Maharaj Ji I've pinned to the wall.

There is a glorious sun, not the sun you see in the sky, but a sun which is within ourselves, and which is much brighter, much, much, much brighter than the sun you see in the sky.

I've been building it up. Look at his face. Concentrate. Close the eyes. I managed it for fourteen minutes at the end of the first week. On Sunday I managed sixteen minutes, and by Wednesday I was up to twenty-two. Tonight, with my mum gone, I will try to make it to half an hour's meditation. I get myself organized. Stop time. Be present. I don't want to be in the school world any more. I want to go with them, away from Mandy Brown and the wearisome school day. Away from the bristling, spotty-skinned teachers and the smell of the toilets. Two fingers on top of my eyeballs, another finger in the middle of my forehead, and count my breath. Then I drop my hands and count. One two three four. Look at the Y-crack on the ceiling. I glance at the clock: 7.48 p.m. I close my eyes. Wait. When I open them again, it is 7.53.

Stopping thoughts is to sort of die. Become nothing. This is why sleep can be scary, why little ones cry out at bedtime, fear it. But I also have another secret. Something strange has happened to my vision since I've started meditating and pressing my eyes. I haven't been able to see the blackboard at school for ages, but now, I am sure, everything is brighter. The light has changed, though I still can't read the words the teacher puts up. I can see words imprinted on the inside of my vision. Like VIETNAM. NO TO THE BLOODY WAR.

Y-crack in the ceiling. Breathe. Concentrate. I do this for some time – suspended seconds, breath in, breath out – and as usual images and people from my life come into my head: Mum, Dave, Dad, Mandy Brown, Gemma, Bill, my English teacher, the dog. They march through my head. Dad says they are not real. They are an illusion. I am itchy and my ankle bone hurts. I carry on, letting the itch and the images of the people I know float away. Bob, bob, bob, bob, they mean nothing. I am floating.

Time – still. Dad taught me another technique. Breathing: so-hum, sooo for the in-breath, hummmm for the out-breath.

Oh, Maharaj Ji, I love you I love you. (Question: if it is all an illusion, like a magic show, then can I love?)

Then a new thing happens. My mind is very awake. Zip. Like when I eat ice cream. Even though my eyes are closed, and I can't shut out the light. A moon shape of light is inside my eyelid. I rub my eye, but then my hand feels weird, as if it isn't mine. I see jigsaw pieces on my skin, magpie feathers, then I flop my hand back down. I blink and blink. A shape like the drawing of a new moon is there.

I blink harder but it won't go. Everything that was too bright is now completely dark. Am I blind? I rub my eyes. When I open them again I can see. But the light is wrong and the shadows too filmy. I walk along the landing, holding on to the wall, then go downstairs. I can see, but everything is different. I pick up the phone in the dining room. The number for my dad's work is sellotaped to the wall. If I get close to it, I can read the numbers. I call, ask for him, and after a long wait he comes to the phone.

'Sue? You okay?'

I lick a tear that has rolled down to my mouth. 'I was… doing it, the techniques, you know, and then I couldn't stop, it filled my eyes with a moon-shape and then I couldn't see properly, like I was a bit blind.'

'Blind? What's happening now? Can you see?'

'I can, but it feels weird.'

'Where's Mum, is she there? Dave okay?'

'Yeah, he's in bed. Mum's not here.'

'She's not there? What?'

'No.' As I say that it shifts again, and the light returns to the inside of my eyes. 'Dad, it's like I can't get it out of my eyeballs.' I slump to the floor, stretching the coiled telephone wire as far as it will go. Now it isn't just light around me, but intense colour. I put my finger on my wrist. It is as if the colours push into my eyes in the same rhythm as my heartbeat. 'Maybe it's my blood? Heart? Dad? Am I dying?'

'What? Sue? Sue, are you there?'

I push the phone to my ear. 'Yeah, Dad.'

'Where's Mum? Has she gone to the shop or something?'

Wetness on my face, around my nose. The colours turn into a tunnel, like a train, as if lights are passing me, and I can't tell if I am moving or not. 'She's out. Yoga. Bill.'

'What?'

I press my head on the floor to stop the feeling of a train swooshing around. I can't stop the lights though. I drop the phone.

From a faraway place, I hear my dad's voice. 'I'm coming home now, I'm coming home now.'

His face is close. His breath smells of Fisherman's Friends. The optician shines his torch to the back of my eyeball and makes me look at a dot and letters. I know I am failing the test and underachieving and am worthless. I keep apologizing. 'You don't have to say sorry for your eyesight,' he says.

'What are the lights in your eyes when you press on your eyelids?' I ask him.

He leans back, turns away from me. 'What do you mean?' He is writing things down on a clipboard. He looks up.

'When you press on your eyelids, swirly lights.'

'Oh, phosphenes,' he says.

'How do you spell that?'

He strings the letters out for me. 'Nothing to worry about, perfectly normal.'

A woman pulls open a drawer. I have a choice of blue or pink. I put the blue glasses on my nose. 'Is it nice to see finally?' she says.

'I suppose so.'

'Are you sure you don't want the pink ones?'

I try them. Pink next to my red hair makes me want to be sick. 'I'd rather have the blue.'

She is disapproving, shaking her head and looking around for my mum, who has wandered off.

Later, wearing the glasses, I look up the word 'phosphenes' in the dictionary: *A sensation of a ring or spot of light produced by pressure on the eyeball or direct stimulation of the visual system other than by light.*

I copy it out neatly in my exercise book. It's just light and light and light and light and light and light and light.

'Listen,' I say to my dad.

We're in my room. I have my new glasses on. I press PLAY on my tape recorder. I installed it in the kitchen one night when Dad was working a shift. I left it under the table, and Bill and my mum didn't notice as they talked about feelings they shouldn't have. *I just want to get away from everything, you know*, she said. *I'm sick of this. This is a shit, shit, too-small life. They need too much. I want more*, she said.

I can give you that, he said.

My journey is a higher one. Sue just wants me to be around her. Talk to her. She's clingy. She gets everywhere, always watching me. This is the wrong life. She is stopping us.

Dad sits with his back to me in my bedroom, listening. His beard is long again. I can't see his face, just the curve of his back and the cable-knit pattern on his shoulders. I don't know if it is a jumper my mum knitted or a bought one. It seems too neat to be one of hers, I think.

My auntie keeps trying to phone. 'It's dead,' she says. 'Why is your phone off, Sue?'

The rough feel of a dog's tongue on my ankle. My auntie's mongrel, Bess, is licking me. Her kids are in bed and we have outstayed our welcome. We were dropped off earlier to play with our cousins, but no one has come to pick us up.

She is agitated. 'Come on, I'll drive you home.' She leaves her kids in bed and bundles us into the back of her Ford Fiesta.

The lights are off in our house, and Mum takes ages to answer the door. Mum says there is a letter on each of our beds from Dad, who has gone. She talks and moves robotic- ally, thanks my auntie, goes to her bedroom and closes the door. Dave and I run up to our bedrooms.

Dear Sue, mine says, *as you know by now, I've had to go. I love you and Dave and Mum most of all of anything in the whole world. I know I haven't told you that very much in the past, but it is true. I know I should have told you and I don't know why I didn't. Maybe it's because I am unhappy with myself. Anyway, I have had to leave because I want to find a really good place to*

*live and find a job that I don't mind doing and a way of life that
is nice. I won't be able to afford a farm with lots of dogs and stuff
like you would love to have and I would love you to have but
maybe I will find something just as good and that's what I am
trying to do. I want to find something good for us all. I love you
a lot and know you have got problems of your own with friends
and school and with being a kid because I did when I was a kid,
and nobody seemed to understand me either. But I understand
and I hope you can understand about me. I am sorry about the
£3.50 the other day it hurt me more than you, but I did...*

I go to my mum's room and bang on the door.

'Go away, Sue, I haven't got the strength tonight.'

Dave comes out of his room, stands next to me, blinking.
We both stand there. 'Can we come in, sleep next to you?'
I say.

'Go away, Sue.'

'Please.'

We are in the doorway. All the lights are on. She turns
her back to us in the bed, but we climb in anyway. We have
no shame. We're like dogs who have been hit and who come
back with a wag. Dave one side, me on the other. The sheets
smell of the cleaning fluid she uses at the old people's home.
Under the covers, in the heat, with my mum sobbing into
the pillow and Dave sucking his thumb, I know I won't sleep.

I go downstairs and sit cross-legged in front of the picture
of Maharaj Ji. I close my eyes. I am a microcosm, something
tiny, and yet my actions cause reactions. Maharaj Ji's eyes
glow. *This is what happens when you don't love the Guru with
a pure true heart. This is what happens when you are a liar,*

the eyes say. *Your fault, you dirty, shitty little girl. This is what happens when you trap a voice and use it as evidence.*

The kitchen smells of toast, the air is thick with kettle steam and smoke. I make toast and soup for Mum as now I can do matches and the cooker. Gas ring high. Gas ring low. I can do boiled eggs and crackers and I ask for money so I can get KitKats and things from the shop. Cornflakes. Jam.

I keep awake because it's the night-time you do it. *I can't carry on,* you say. *I can't do it. I just want to die.*

Mum's in bed, smoking, and won't come out. She cries and cries. 'I just want to die,' she says. I assess the risk. It would be a knife, I suppose, so I hide the kitchen knives under the dog food tray. The only thing that calms me is the layering of the housebuilding on the walls of the coal shed. I copy them out from the catalogue.

Expandable House.

Personal Politics of building your own home, Hillside homestead.

Owner-built home. Engineered home. From the ground up.

She roams the house at night. Stands in the kitchen smoking. One night I go down and look at her. She moves a bag of knitting off a chair and puts it on the table. She stands up then sits down. 'What do you do in your coal shed, Sue?'

'Think about building a house.' I'm taking out the house-building instructions one by one.

'You think a house is going to save you?' she says, screeching the kitchen chair back and turning to the sink. She runs water from the taps but doesn't find a glass or a cup. I walk over and turn off the tap. I stare at her. *I am eleven*, I want to say. *It's too much and it's not my fault*. But these words aren't manageable. She can't see me, I don't think, and if she does, she doesn't like what she sees. I flatten myself against the kitchen wall. I hold on to the door handle for strength. I wish Dad were here to step between us. Just us now. Nothing in between. It is unclear who is the grown-up. I whisper a word to myself: danger.

I hear the gremlin-voice again. 'You want your mammy feck feck and you cannot have her she's ours. You want her to die. You could shove her with your little fingers over the edge of the tracks, couldnay ya couldnay ya we know. Be done with it! Be free of it! Go on with your little words and your houses made of matchsticks. Be done with her and be free. We know ya secret, little feck.'

Personal Effects

I felt bad about interrupting Tony's life and grubbing about in his past. I got an email from him a week after meeting him in Bianchi's.

I got hold of Bill's address, it said. *He lives in Stockport. Here it is, and his landline, though he doesn't have a mobile.*

I emailed Tony back, something generic and polite. I had a lot of questions for him, a lot more to say. *You are the only person who understands how I feel*, I wrote. *I feel invaded. Possessed? Do you have this feeling of gremlins in and around you? You mentioned aliens, maybe that is your version?*

He emailed an enormous message. It was a mash-up of Gibran's *The Prophet*, the Upanishads and the *Hatha Yoga Pradipika*.

I didn't reply, and I didn't hear from him again.

It was half-term and I needed to get out of the house. I had been manically buying curtains and soft furnishings on eBay, but all the jobs remained unfinished. I wanted to make our home a pleasant sanctuary for my family, but I didn't seem to have the gene. I'd pulled off wallpaper with a view to redecorating and said the kids could write on the walls. We went to town. *Bum. Penis. Cock.* Then, of course, I did not re-wallpaper. All day the kids sprawled about on their devices, spreading homework and socks everywhere. I snarled at everyone, 'Clear it up! We all live here!'

There was endless debris thrown into the bin: broken pencil sharpeners, Post-it notes covered in dog hair and books with their covers ripped off. I shouted at the kids to pull up their feet so I could sweep past them.

Purge! Purge!

I could never get control over the washing-up or the cramped back garden. Instead, all my brain wanted to do was write, draw and type. I was itching in my skin. My scalp was often hot. I developed a sniff and then it went again. I was agitated in my soul. I had been in this place of anxiety before in my life. I knew I needed to isolate myself to get through it.

My husband understood that I needed to go to Crewe. I hadn't been back for years and I wanted to have a look around for some undetermined project. I remembered, too, that Nana had left me some letters. They were stored at my auntie's house.

He was sceptical. 'Can't you just Google Earth it?'

I invented a paper I was writing and a deadline and said I was going to ensconce myself in a Travelodge to get it done. Forty-eight hours. It might as well be Crewe. I felt guilty leaving my husband with the kids, but I went anyway. What I didn't tell him was that I thought the kids would be safer without me around for a while because I was feeling… and the only way I could find to articulate this to myself was *unstable.*

*

I was calmer in the privacy of the hotel. My generic room faced the car park, and with the blinds down no one could see in. I wiped off my make-up and spread out all my stuff on the bed. I flicked the TV on and turned it down low. I turned on my laptop and pulled out a pad of A4 lined paper. Just a cheap lot, but what I needed. For an hour or so I let my pen draw endless pointless doodles in circles to get my breathing to feel normal.

Some people drink. Some people cut. Some use sex or cycling or exercise. My secret shame felt so weird that I had told no one. Not even my husband. I have since read that it's called *hypergraphia*: an inability to stop drawing or writing. Maybe it's a real thing. Maybe it's not. All I knew is that I could not stop writing. On walls or skin, it didn't matter. On paper. On the floor.

For the next few hours, I flipped from screen to paper. Lists. Bullet points. Repetitions of words. At one point, despite having quit a decade ago, I decided to smoke and walked out in the drizzle to find a shop. The street in Crewe was both familiar and alien. The railway terraces had doors that opened from the living room directly on to the street. A man stood on a kerb looking at me. He had a lead in his hand but no dog at the end of it. As I wandered, I analysed: did I feel at home? Was this a place I belonged in? Drooping England flags, bins out for recycling.

The name Crewe is derived from the Welsh word *criu*, meaning weir or crossing. A transit point, famous for its railway station and not much else.

I walked around the town centre for a little while, trying to remember it, trying to feel connected to it, but I couldn't find a way back. A ring road I couldn't understand. Taxis in a row. Posters. The marketplace, but shut up so just the frames of the stalls.

For the rest of the evening I consumed cigarettes and Diet Coke. I tried to run a bath, but the water came out lukewarm. I let my phone battery run down. I slept for a bit, despite the caffeine, and it was dark when I woke up. I sat up and was about to go to the loo when I heard, or rather felt, a presence. Like a cat scratching to get in. Only different.

I realized that this was why I had come. I was waiting for it.

Holding the pen loosely in my hand, I started to write, stuff I'd googled earlier about Crewe.

This town, I wrote, *was built for workers of the Grand Junction Railway. They were shipped in from Liverpool, Ireland, Wales and Lancashire. It was founded on company paternalism: the factory owners paid them pennies, just enough for the pub, and workers gave them their lives.*

Scratches. Scrape. A nibble at my skin. I could feel it, or them, biting me.

The main investor in the town's company, John Moss, had sugar plantations in Demerara. The train tracks of empire made by the factories weren't just laid by the skin of workers but also drew on the blood, hair and skeletons of slaves.

I continued writing. I wrote to fend it off, but also to draw it in. *Train stories in the family: Irish Nana at Crewe station with her kids (my mum and her brother and sister) in the early sixties, when a woman tried to give her a baby – 'Take it, take it, take it!' – but Nana refused. Great-Grandad was a train driver. My other grandad was a ticket collector, and my dad was a brakeman for a while. Nana was sent to Crewe from Monaghan, Ireland, as a twenty-year-old to work in Radway Green Munitions in the war. Grandad came to Crewe for a Rolls-Royce factory job after being demobbed in the sixties. And underneath them all, train tracks built on slavery.*

It was close. It was on the roof, with scratchy feet. It climbed down the drainpipe and scrabbled at the window. It picked out window putty and poked out bricks.

'In a hotel room, are you? Traitor.' The words were very clear.

It moved slowly across the carpet, creeping along.

'Slut slut slut traitor.'

I'd been waiting for it for years; I'd known it was coming. The ink from my pen drained out; the link between my head and page was immediate. A cross between a gremlin and Maharaj Ji. How stupid, and yet it was real. I put down my pen and stood up. I moved around the room in squares to get away from it.

'Pick up your pen,' it said. So I did. The gremlin-Maharaj Ji was close to me now, breathing near my head, pulling at my skin. 'Uh uh,' it said, 'not possible. No place for you.' There was a feeling in my skin when I got close to it – a vibrancy, a truth. A spilling of the shit. The sense of the nearness of that came over me; it felt like a curse or brainwashing.

My dad, and all his brothers, beaten by my grandad. All of them flinching, crying when he came in, hiding and weeing themselves. The belt. The slipper. The clout. Box ears. Shouts of, 'You'll be for it. Just wait till he gets home.' Great-Grandad was brought up in a children's home by nuns in Ireland and beaten he was.

What does working in a factory for an industrial empire do to a body?

I paused. Listened to its presence. I could feel it in the room. It was reading what I was writing, peeping over my shoulder or from inside my head.

Crewe Works at its height employed over 20,000 people; due to the vast expanse of the work, much of the landscape was and is still shaped by the railway… heritage groups did not succeed in preserving the wall.

It was in my fingertips and it was part of the pen. It was a fluid line from brain to imprint.

'Fingers come, they pick you apart,' it said. I shivered. This phrase was familiar to me. I wrote to fend it off. My skin seemed to open, as if being peeled back. I thought I might be sick.

Welsh Nana skivvying, cleaning, scrubbing. Irish side, postmen, barmaids serving people and the military. Giving, offering, handing over the years of their life in service to others and making it a virtue. Dad in a factory to this day. Working these jobs is exhausting and enacts a form of violence on the body. My dad's hands shaking, the tinnitus…

But it didn't work. It fully entered my brain, as it had done at other points in my life, and I lay on the bed as this gremlin took over my eyes, thoughts, skin and soul.

*

I woke early the next morning after a weird, blackout sleep. I had written on everything I could find in the room. The menu, the DO NOT DISTURB sign, toilet paper, paper towels. Repetition of words related to Crewe Works mainly: the Melts, the erecting, signal and paintwork shops, the drawing office. STOP THE SLAUGHTER! VIETNAM! I stood up and went to the bathroom. I tried to speak to myself, but my mouth was too dry. I looked about three years older than I had the previous day.

On the floor of the bathroom, written sideways across pages and pages of A4 lined paper, was a letter to myself debating whether I should or should not kill myself. Repetitive and tedious. *Do it. Why not. No point not. Kids. Do it. Mother. Do it.* And here I was, looping, in and out of a behaviour that wasn't entirely mine. That somehow had trapped me, as if I were in a kaleidoscope or a paperweight forever.

I walked to Queens Park, a Victorian municipal park on the edge of the rec, to clear my head. So much had changed. The main arteries of Crewe roads were the same.

As I walked, the gremlin-Maharaj Ji's voice rumbled. 'Become one. Become whole, and I don't mean "hole", I mean whole! Complete! Or maybe even become that hole, so that Guru Maharaj Ji can come through in your life. Surrender.'

I lapped the park once, but I couldn't find the way out into the rec. I felt lonely and disconnected, like a kid with a den but no one to invite in. My husband and children were in a far-off realm. I hadn't turned my phone back on yet.

The gremlin-Maharaj Ji was near me at all times, touching my ankles or hanging back, jeering.

It repeated pat phrases from the tapes. 'You are just a cockroach crawling around in the fabric of a rug. You can't see the big picture, the bigger design. I can. You need me to see the embroidery and the meaning.'

'Not real,' I said. I knew there was a risk in talking to it in my head. A conversation might validate it. Better to dumb it away, numb it away. Better to drink extra wine, travel to a Buddhist retreat, run seventeen marathons, better to do anything than deal with this presence. 'Why are you following me?'

Gravel underfoot. I remembered cycling along here decades ago, the rumble over the gravel making my hands vibrate and itch on the handlebars, the hardness of a bicycle seat in the crotch, the balance.

'Because I can,' it said.

'I need you to go away.'

'No whore dirty no. I am sticking near you, sticky like finger in your mouth like bits of dribble and spit on you can't move away from me I know it all. When those vultures start closing in and the rattler gets awful close to attacking and you drop a few tears and someone is here. The feet. You turn around and there is Guru Maharaj Ji.'

I exited the park through the gate that led to the rec. It was all still the same. I had that sense, again, of looking for something. What was it?

A person cycled close to me, swerving to pass. Don't speak out loud, I thought. I knew then what I was looking for. The bunker Gemma and I used to call the Museum. The gremlin-Maharaj Ji laughed. 'You'll never find it, ever,' it said. 'It's gone, dirty girl, gone. Here is Maharaj Ji whispering: Come here, I can help.'

My auntie was an unsettled person with a transitory feeling about her, as if she was in the wrong place even though it was her house. I'd disturbed her afternoon of attacking a bramble bush in the corner of her garden. Her wrists were covered with scratches, similar to those from a cat when play has turned nasty. Nana had insisted that the letters were for me.

'I don't know why she wanted you to have them, but she did. They're letters about Stanley, I think,' my auntie said, and a shadow came over her. It was my uncle. 'Do you remember that time, Sue?'

I did remember that time, the shock of it. Our phone wasn't cut off, and it rang. My mum slumped backwards against the wall and let the phone fall to the floor. Nana went to bed and wouldn't come out of the bedroom because her son, my Uncle Stanley, the one in the RAF, stationed in Berlin, guarding a wall for Thatcher, was dead.

Extracting myself from my auntie, I went back to the Travelodge. I read one of the letters of condolence from Flight Lieutenant J. Founders, RAF Lyneham.

I have been appointed by my Station Commander to look after your son's personal effects and I am now writing to explain exactly what will happen. After his belongings have been collected and listed by me, they will be sent (apart from any bulky items which will remain here for the time being) to the Standing Committee of

Adjustment at Innsworth, Gloucester, where they will be checked against my list and properly stored until the Ministry of Defence is able to authorize release.

I thought of the words 'personal effects' and tried to imagine his last thought as the metal and the screeching sound came close and then were on him. Shoes. Watch. Jumper. Folded and arranged neatly by the side of the track.

I knew my husband was worried and that I should go back for the kids, but I begged another day. The gremlins were still near, scratching when I paused. Scratching when I showered. It sometimes helped to lie on the carpeted floor, but I noticed that if I wrote factually, controlled, rational information about Maharaj Ji the voices calmed. If I spoke to my kids on the phone the noises went away completely.

'What's going on?' my husband said.

'Just let me work through this. I'm sorry.'

Recently I had given a lecture on 'the counterculture'. It was hard to gauge what my students thought of American military recordings of lost children being blasted into the jungle in Vietnam. I taught Didion's essays and tried to show how an epoch, or a series of beliefs, eventually becomes a caricature of itself, but that didn't make it meaningless.

Scratch scratch.

I wrote: *Maharaj Ji rented the Houston Astrodome for 'Millennium '73', billed as 'the most significant and holy event in the history of mankind', and promoted himself as God...*

I'd asked Mum about it all directly once. I remembered she'd said: 'I don't know, there were a lot of people, we used to meet in hotels. Big conference hotels, with signs up and everyone in the lobby looking at us as if we were freaks. We had to be careful who we talked to because Mam and my sister thought we were brainwashed. They thought they were an American cult, so we got secretive.'

Scratchy noises. Itch.

Maharaj Ji, son of Param Hans Ram Yogiraj Shri, a guru who oversaw the vast Prem Nagar ashram called the 'City of Love'. Hans Ram's guru was Swarupanand, from the Advait Mat lineage of northern India. In 1923 Swarupanand taught Hans Ram the extremely secret, mystical yoga practices called kriyas *that supposedly achieved almost supernatural results. In 1926, Swarupanand instructed Hans Ram to share them with the world, and baby Prem inherited this mission. Later, he split with his controlling mum and went off on his own journey, bringing all the druggy, thirsty Westerners with him.*

This seemed to help.

I emailed Prem Rawat's current organization, Words of Peace, again requesting an interview. He was now an 'inspirational life coach and spiritual leader'. I wanted to ask him how he felt about telling so many people not to work. To meditate all day. That stuff was evil and careers were wrong. I tried from a different email account. *I was wondering if you have an archive I could access…*

An intolerable, ancient tiredness splintered through me. Like the exhaustion that comes during the baby years. I remembered the Joan Didion essay about the mum giving her daughter acid and peyote. Where was that daughter now?

What I really wanted to know was what was behind my mum's lifelong suicidal impulse. It couldn't have been just because of Maharaj Ji. A more knotted, gruesome death wish? I was endlessly trapped in trying to figure out how I could unpick it all.

I checked my emails. I'd been corresponding with an academic who specialized in the adverse effects of meditation on children. *There's almost no data*, he said, *on the impact of meditation on children, for obvious reasons. We have research on light and hallucination experiences in meditation, and old research on sensory deprivation, but nothing since the 1970s. I would be most interested to hear your childhood experiences. This is a gap. It is lacking in scientific enquiry, despite mindfulness and mediation being omnipresent these days…*

I leaned back on the bed. The voices had stopped. I texted my husband an apology, but he was busy rushing the kids around to clubs and didn't, or couldn't, reply.

Do you wanna become rich? I can make you the richest possible man… Mind you, I don't have the currency of dollars or pounds. I have the perfect currency, which is called Knowledge.

Council House, Early 1980s

The gruff, kind Yorkshire nurse with thick brown freckles makes me open my mouth and stick out my tongue while she shoves a thermometer down my throat. 'Fever,' she says. 'You've got to go home.' I've been hot since my dad left, but this is the first time anyone's noticed. She flicks through my file and picks up the phone. 'I'll call your mum to see if she can come and get you.'

I sit on the squishy chair, staring at the floor.

'That's weird,' she says. 'No tone.'

'It might be off.'

'Off?'

'Cut off.'

'Right.' She frowns and examines the paperwork in front of her. 'I don't have any other numbers. Where does she work?'

'I don't know the name of it. An old people's home.'

The nurse rubs her hands along her substantial thighs, sits down in the swivel chair and shunts herself across the room, panting a little. She drops gum that I hadn't seen her chewing into the wastepaper basket. 'Your dad?'

'He's not around at the moment.'

'Righto. Well. Are there any other numbers we can call? You can't stay here. Any relatives?'

I think. I don't know either of my nanas' phone numbers. Or my auntie's. I shake my head.

'Any close family friends?'

I don't know Bill's surname or what town his number might come under in the book. 'Gemma Williams,' I say. 'She lives across the road. She's in my year.'

The nurse hauls open an enormous green filing cabinet drawer and flicks through the files. She phones the number. 'Could Suzanne Joinson be picked up? Can't get through to her parents. She has a fever, needs to go to bed, lots of fluids, sweat it out. Perhaps some paracetamol.' There is a pause. 'Thank you.'

There is a special smell in nurses' rooms, I think.

'Okay, someone called Mickey is collecting you...' She glances again at the file. 'There's no other next of kin. He's a family friend, right?'

I nod.

'Okay, get your bag and coat and go and wait in reception for him. And try not to breathe on anyone.'

On the back of Mickey's motorbike, the wind whips up my fever nicely. Both hot and cold, I am light, feminine, ill, and a bit like a cat as I press against his back. He drives as far as the corner near the end of our road but doesn't turn down it.

'Enjoying the ride?'

'Yeah.'

'Want to go back to the house or keep going?'

My teeth are juddering; I have just about enough strength to hold on to his tracksuit jacket with my hands. I cling tightly to him to stay on. 'Keep going,' I say. I like moving. I rest my hot cheek on his back as he revs the engine of his motorbike. He takes the road that curves along the back of the park. He turns into the track that leads to the rec, where men race remote-controlled cars on Sundays and teenagers mooch about on BMXs riding down the remains of the bomb craters. It is empty, as the citizens of the world are about their business. Mickey bumps the bike on to a field and lifts me down, pulls off his helmet and unclips mine. I squint across the green space. It's over on the other side where the concrete bunker is that I go in with Gemma.

'Jesus,' he says. 'You're really shaking.'

The fever moves from cold shivers to boiling. I am sweaty everywhere. He puts his hand on my forehead.

'Oh dear, hope you're not catching.' He smiles, scraping his boot on the earth and grass. He scans the field behind us and puts his gloves in the compartment at the back of his bike. I look around too. There is nobody, nothing, just sky and grass. He opens his arms. 'Would a hug help?'

I don't think I want to hug him, but I step forward.

'I think a hug would help. Come here.' This time it is a statement, not a question. He pats his leg. I follow his instruction. When I am close, he pulls me towards him. I come up to his chest area, just below. He hugs me in tight and squeezes his arms around me, just as my dad does sometimes, but this is harder and he is taller. He puts his head down, kisses me on the top of mine and says, 'You feel delicious, a little shivery.'

I switch from hot to cold. Ice cold. I am freezing. I think he is kissing my head and putting his hand on my neck, but I can't tell exactly. His hand is inside my school uniform shirt, fingers tapping like the birds do when they draw the worms up. He rubs the tip of his finger over my belly button, then something comes up in me, strong and bilious-tasting. It rises through my throat and out of my mouth. I puke on his chest, down his trousers, over the whole of him. I retch until it is just a string of liquid coming out of my mouth.

'Jesus fucking Christ.' He lurches away from me and looks down at the mass of gunk covering him.

I wipe the liquid from my mouth, step away from him and run.

'Where are you going?' he shouts. 'Come back.'

I run towards the centre of the rec, my school shoes going deep into the muddy grass. Mickey's voice sounds like a cow's, a moan-call. I carry on running, and after a while I hear a motorbike engine, and when I finally turn to look back, he isn't there any more.

They don't notice I'm back from school early. I've been walking around and around the park until I can't walk any more. Fever filters through my body, sometimes making me so cold it's like my skin is going to fall off. I think: I will tell her I'm ill, I will tell her I was sick on Mickey's jacket. I think: I'll tell Dad when I see him when I speak to him next when he comes back.

*

His letters come on lined spiral-bound journalist notepaper in white envelopes.

I am in Canterbury at the moment and it's quite nice here and tomorrow I am going to see if there are any jobs here for the likes of me... The old Beetle is still putting along just about but I expect it to give up at any minute it's getting a bit smelly though with me living in it. Haven't found a job yet, but here I am sitting in the Beetle looking through the paper. Going to the phone box in a minute to call up about a van driver job. About the only thing I can do – driving. Anyway, I'll have to go and find a quiet country spot to park and spend the night now, so I'll write again soon.

I carry his letters everywhere and at lunchtime I read them in the library. The carpet is a reassuring moss green, occasionally stained with old chewing gum. The plastic seats have long since come loose on their hinges. There are booths you can sit at to work and be alone. My favourite is in the corner next to 'MUSIC THEORY'. I sometimes get a map of England to follow his journey *'looking for a new home and life for us'*. I look out at the dishrag sky of Crewe. I try to believe this. I lean my head on my palm. There is a snuffling near my ear, and I jump as Mandy Brown snatches my letters.

I twist around. 'Give them back,' I call. Her pretty face is sweaty with laughter. She reverses away and looks at the paper. She begins reading bits out to people in the library.

'That's mine.' I move towards her. She backs herself behind a table. She reads out: *'The old Beetle is still putting along just about but I expect it to give up at any minute it's getting a bit smelly though with me living in it.'*

'Why is your dad living in a beetle?' Then she figures it out. 'Your dad is living in his car?'

She laughs and moves towards the library doors. I run after her, screaming. A dinner lady twists around, along with every other person nearby. Mandy calls out another line: '*Write me real letters, Sue, not boring ones like you write to pen-pals. Tell me how you really feel.* Creepy!'

I run at her.

'Tell me how you feeeeel, Sue,' she shouts. Kids watch, rucksacks dropped to the floor, jaws opening, eyes widening.

'I'm living in a car Sueeeeeeeeee. I'm a gypsy. I'm a tramp. I'm a disgusting homeless person. Your dad's a homeless person.' I see it before it happens: broken nose and her skin peeled back, like the coiled edge of a slice of raw bacon. I lurch towards her, ready to crush her sweaty face. I get as far as her hair, my fingers poking in to get to her skull, about to raise her head and smash it down.

A man's hand grabs my shoulder and hauls me up. He wraps his arms around me. I can't stop screaming. I try to bite him, then wrestle away and scrabble about on the floor, grabbing bits of my dad's letter.

'Give me the letters,' I sob out. Most of the paper is wet, and my dad's handwriting is stained and ruined. Two teachers are there, and the man. Mandy shouts that I am a psycho-crazy mental bitch. The man holds me again, and I can smell his skin. I even get the trace of the whiskers on his face, and he drags me away backwards.

I am put in a cupboard-room that has a photocopier and a wall of files and am told to sit still and cool off. I itemize what I see in front of me to stop myself from crying: pink folder, stapler, boxes of paper, paper cutter, plastic envelopes for A4 paper, three green biros, one blue, five red, and no pencils. No pencils. I keep repeating it over and over again. No pencils.

Without Dad our house feels as if the door is always open and won't close properly. No more Bombay mix. No more lentil stew. Instead we have chips and eggs about three nights a week. Or tins of tomato soup and rice pudding. Mum no longer slices vegetables into a great big raw salad. No more dried banana slices or tofu. Now we are allowed crisps and KitKats.

She's developed sore spots on her elbows and wrists. She rubs cream into them, but the sores won't stop coming and are spreading to her nose, forehead, neck and chest. I add a new word, psoriasis, to the list of things I am to blame for. I have to stay at home for a week because of my antisocial behaviour and write an English composition each day. I sit on the windowsill and watch middle-of-the-day people, life's losers: the disengaged, unemployed, the knackered mums with pushchairs and the uninvolved. Mum's at work. Dave's at school. I lie on the rug in the living room and count the spiderweb trails on the ceiling.

She moves around the house at night, smoking. I don't know who she is speaking to. Sometimes there is a bottle of wine near the fireplace in the morning, about half of it drunk.

I tell her I'm hungry all day when she is out. She pushes a tin towards me.

'What is it?'

'Spam,' she says. Then she puts another one down. 'Corned beef.' I've never seen anything like them before. They have a key that twists to peel open the lid. 'You can have it on bread, and it'll keep you full until I get back. I used to have it as a kid, it's fine.'

I pull on the key and peel back the metal lid. 'It's meat.' Mum shrugs.

'Are we not vegetarian any more?'

She presses a finger into her cheek and sighs. 'I don't know what we are any more.'

Dave has always loved going to our grandparents' houses to get pork chops, sausages and roast chicken, any meat he can, but I've never eaten any. He comes up to the counter, sniffs the corned beef and makes a gagging noise.

'See,' I say. 'Even he doesn't want it. I'm not eating that, totally gross.'

Mum's mouth is a thin line. Her hair vibrates with a new level of angriness. 'Come on, Dave, got to get you to school. It's that or toast.'

'I don't understand what's happening. Why are we eating meat?' I say. 'Or should I say dog food?'

She takes the corned beef tin and holds it up in front of me, shakes it, and the meat falls and splats on to the floor. It smells disgusting. Then she gets the mug that she's just slurped coffee from and smashes it on the floor. Everything stinks of coffee and the horrible meat. She turns to me, her face pale. 'It's good enough for me. But not you, eh?' She grabs Dave and shoves his arm in his coat.

'Mum,' I say.

'Yes?' But she is dragging Dave to the door, away, not looking.

'Mum.' I shout it at her back. She turns around. 'When I had my eyes tested, I told the optician about the flashing lights in the eyes, the fingers on the eyelids when you press them, and he said it's just an optical illusion.'

She stares at me. 'What are you talking about?' With the front door open and the cold coming in, she pushes Dave's other arm into his blue coat.

'He told me the name.' I say. 'I wrote it down. Phosphenes. Lights that you see when you press your eyelids.'

'I don't know what you're on about. We're going now.' She tugs Dave out on to the step and slams the door shut. It is 8.55, and I have until 3.30 on my own. It's only Tuesday.

He smells of tobacco and dirt when he hitch-hikes to see us for the weekend. It's hard to meditate in a car, he says, but soon he will get back into the rhythm. He's come from a place called Pevensey Bay and is skinny, a bit whiffy. It's on the south coast and he's found a temporary job working as a van driver. 'You know, Sue,' he says, 'the south is better. Everything will be better there.' We play Escape from Colditz all afternoon.

Later, at bedtime, I ask him if he still believes in Maharaj Ji and the Knowledge.

'Of course,' he says. 'Now more than ever.' He gives me a weird look.

'Does Mum hate us?'

'It's very complicated,' he says.

'Tell me about the Nectar technique,' I say. Then I can go with him to the Infinite.

He shakes his head. 'No, it's not safe, it's not easy, you have to work hard to get to it, to understand. Why do you want to know so much?'

I don't know how to explain that I have nothing else to believe and so I want the magic techniques to glue our world back together.

'All right,' he said, looking at my face. 'We'll go through it.'

It is called Tasting Nectar in meditation, and the Indian name is Khechari. We are sitting in the living room, practising.

Firstly, I have to collect spit in my mouth, hold it there, then drink it down. Next, I curl my tongue back towards the back of my throat. Then breathe in and out for fifteen minutes. I am supposed to taste a magical sweet taste in my mouth.

'What do you mean, natural sweet flavour?' My spit tastes of nothing, of the orange squash I had a bit ago, maybe. Of crisps.

Then I have to poke my tongue out and pull on it to stretch it as long as possible.

Dad lights the smoky coal fire and a couple of candles. It is past nine, and there is no sign of Mum. She's gone out while he is here. Prearrangement.

'Some of the mahatmas… instructors, sorry, say to tug your tongue every day to "lengthen" it.' He waggles his tongue at me. 'The gurus used to gradually sever the frenulum, cut this bit here that connects the tongue to the rest of the mouth, but that doesn't happen any more, though it is in the *Hatha Yoga Pradipika.*'

'How do you spell that, Dad?' I write it down.

'The Maharaj Ji version is to press the tongue right back. You can even use your fingers to shove them further down and connect,' he says. He demonstrates the technique and with his mouth full of hand. 'Oungg gghug gh,' he says. 'Sousnss sss houug ggg.'

There is the sound of a car outside and a door slamming. Mum lets herself in. We are cross-legged in front of the fire. My eyes are watering. Dad immediately changes. If he was a colour before, red-golden and green, he is now dark grey and black. I walk out. She has stolen him back, and I haven't got the full Nectar secret.

'*Hatha Yoga Pradipika?*'

The *Hatha Yoga Pradipika* from the library is huge. I spend lunchtime flicking through it and find the superpowers. Gazing steadily at a small mark until your eyes fill with tears destroys eye diseases and removes sloth. It's a list of instructions that should be kept secret, like a box of jewellery. I flick through. Reverse ageing and become sixteen again. Blow wind from the anus out through the eyebrows.

I find a chapter on how to cut the tongue.

The *Khecarīvidyā* gives instructions on how to cut the lingual frenulum as a necessary prerequisite for the practice of *khechari mudra: he should take a very sharp, well-oiled and clean blade resembling a leaf of the snuhī plant and cut away a hair's breadth of the lingual frenulum with it. After cutting, he should rub the cut with a powder of rock salt and black myrobalan. After seven days he should again cut away a hair's breadth... After six months the binding tendon at the base of the tongue is destroyed... Then, in six more months, after regular drawing-out of the tongue, my dear, it reaches between the eyebrows... Licking with his tongue the supreme nectar of immortality, amrita, flowing here... the yogi should drink... and with a body as incorruptible as diamond, lives for 100,000 years...*

I sit back in my chair in the library. Is this the secret, then, that my dad is working towards? Living for 100,000 years? And if so, is it the case that Bill and all the other Premies who obviously know the secrets will live that long? It occurs to me that they are vampires.

Home smells green and musty. There's a broken cream cracker on the floor in the hall. Bill is in the kitchen staring into a cardboard box that is on the table.

'Where's Mum?'

'In the garden.'

'Where's Dave?'

'Watching telly.'

There is something off about him, been smoking possibly. Taken something.

I open the back door. Mum is wrapped in a big blanket. It's about to go dark, and there's a drizzle in the air.

'What's happening?'

Bill shoves past me with the box and dumps it on the grass next to Mum. She speaks to Bill as if I'm not there.

'What does it mean?' She sucks heavily on the cigarette.

'Declares himself human?' he says, 'As in, not God.' They are both being extremely weird.

'Well,' Mum says. 'They've been closing the ashrams. You knew that, Bill.' She drops the cigarette on the floor and grinds it into the grass.

'That's gross,' I say. 'Use an ashtray.'

Bill turns and looks at me, then he puts his hands on his knees and bends forwards so that his face is at the same height as mine, and shunts himself very close. He's been around a lot recently. He's 'helping'. 'Critical little person, aren't you? Maybe when you're older you can be a critic. Yeah? Little critic.' He swivels back towards Mum as if forgetting about me instantly.

'What's happening?' I ask.

'Maharaj Ji,' she says, 'has declared himself human. Not the Lord. The One. Perfect Master.'

'What are you supposed to call him now?' I say.

'Ultimate Ruler.'

I laugh. Even Mum laughs and meets my eye, but Bill is fuming.

'Cunt Fucker Fucking Shit,' Bill sighs. He puts his arm around Mum and squeezes her towards him. 'I miss the ashram days. You knew where you were, you got the free tea and the special privileges. Ultimate Ruler is just not as romantic, you know?'

'Yeah,' my mum said, 'but you had to hand over your wage cheque, remember?'

'Still do,' he says.

Dave is watching *He-Man and the Masters of the Universe*. I slump next to him on the sofa.

'The big news, Dave, is that Maharaj Ji isn't God.'

On the telly, Randor, king of Eternia and father of He-Man, peers over the edge of a cliff.

'Not Ultimate Ruler?' he says.

Despite that news, I have made the most progress on the Divine Light one. The tongue one is too difficult.

The letters come. We are moving to a seaside town called Eastbourne, in the south. He is saving money. We will be together. Better.

Saturday morning, I sit up in my bed. Something is different. I look around.

The bed and door are the same. The books are arranged as normal. Clothes are in a heap on the floor. What is different? I rub my eyes. Is it to do with how I see things, colours? But then I realize I am not inside myself. I am looking down at the top of my shoulders, it is as if I am floating up near the ceiling. I move around in bed to shake the creepy feeling, but while my body shunts around, the real me floats above. The bed-me is nothing. I touch my hand, but there is no sense there at all. I can't feel it when I scratch the inside of my palm. I get out of bed and stand up. I bend over and touch the floor, then stretch and put my hands on the top of my head. I lick my lips again. My mouth is dry.

Again, nothing. As if I'm there but not. I'm too terrified to look upwards at myself up there, yet at the same time I am looking down at the physical me. I press my hands on my forehead and squeeze my eyes shut. Try to get back to normal. Here is the room, my bedroom, my life, but it means nothing. I try not to listen, but there is a voice. 'Whatever you pick up, so you become. Because it's all the little *lila*, or play, of mind that brings you into all the confusion and everything of this world. And that's why a man needs the *lila* of the Perfect Master. Because that brings him into something that is completely perfect...'

I move out of my room to get away from the voice.

'Whatever you pick up, so you become. Vietnam. China. India. East. Secret. Go!'

Mum is hoovering downstairs, mid-purge. She's put a row of bin bags full of stuff near the front door. I go to the toilet, pull down my pyjamas, sit on the toilet seat, do a wee. I feel liquid coming out of me, but not its temperature. I am disconnected from the process. Words pop into the space in my head, textually, as if rolling before my eyes and embedded in the thought as it materializes in my brain. *Your words mean nothing. Your thoughts are not your own. You have no choice. It doesn't matter. It's meaningless. It doesn't matter.* I don't say these words out loud, but their pervasive feeling spreads across me. Although I have no emotional connection to the words, I am inside them. It's as if the bit of my brain that understands language has walked away.

I sit on the floor in front of the toilet and wonder if I am invisible. Have I fully disintegrated? I stand up and look in the mirror. I'm there, but my usual feelings, all emotions, are now turned off. Although not really. Because deeper down, in a different place inside me, I'm freaking out. I am panicking. I have a dread feeling. I hear Mum and Dave downstairs having an altercation about something. His stuff on the floor, his toys in the way. I start to cry but I can't feel the emotion of crying, just the wet stick of tears on my skin.

A letter from my dad says *We are going to be together again!* We are on the list for a council house exchange and soon going to Eastbourne, where we will start our new, better life. But the words move on the page.

Eastbourne
Exchange soon
NEW LIFE
Council House – on list

Afterwards, I can't find the school copy of the *Hatha Yoga Pradipika* to return it, and I suspect it has been lost in a purge.

I am sick of Bill in our house. 'We'll be moving soon,' I say to him one afternoon. Not hiding my nasty tone.

Mum sighs. 'All right, Sue.' She turns towards the window. Bill rubs his elbow and organizes his face into an expression of sincerity and understanding, like a school counsellor. He opens his mouth about to lecture me or tell me a long Divine Light Mission-y story. I roll my eyes.

'Don't give me a look like that Sue,' he says, pissed off. 'Cheeky, too cheeky.' I look at him across the kitchen. Mum is at the wall and pings the light switch as it's gone dim outside. Nobody seems to be watching the fire.

I can see well in the kitchen light. It's as if my glasses have strengthened. I blink and see that Bill is a vampire, big and hawklike. Vampires use yoga techniques to live for ten thousand years. His face is made to suck blood, and his scales are barely hidden by the skin. Bill makes his vampire voice soft and pretend-human: 'Listen, Sue, I know you think you're very clever, but…'

Mum puts her hand on his arm. 'Bill, stop it.' She looks nervous, glancing at me. She wipes her mouth with her palm.

'I'm ill,' I say, but nobody hears me. 'There's something wrong with my head.'

'Sue, want to go for a drive with me? So we can chat?' he says.

I shake my head. 'Nope.' No way. No cars with vampires. Bill looks at Mum and raises his eyebrows. 'Driving is less confrontational,' he whispers.

'I can hear you,' I say, 'because I'm standing here.'

'Okay. Go, Sue, go,' my mum says. I shake my head.

'No, I'm ill, can't you see?' I put my hand on my throat. I'm sweating all over, I'm boiling again like I was with Mickey, but her voice is cold.

'You will go and talk to him.'

I shake my head. She starts to vibrate with fury and moves close towards me. 'You will go. Bill just wants to talk to you.' She holds my pigtail and pulls it, sharp. She steps away from me and holds on to the backdoor handle as if that could help her with anything. She puts her head on the wall, and I think: don't look to the walls of this house to hold yourself up, Mother.

Bill's car smells of patchouli. The back seat is crammed with plants, aloe vera and some other spiky-leafed ones. There is soil all over the floor. Kids' cardigans and wellies are shoved in all the car's crevices. A string of evil eye beads hangs from the mirror and taps against the windscreen as he drives.

'Don't you want to know where we're going?'

I don't speak to vampires. He drives towards the Wimpey estate. I sit back in the big leather seat and try to stop myself shivering.

Bill digs around in his coat pocket and pulls out a ready-made rollie. He lights it but doesn't open the window. 'You know, Sue,' he says, 'I've considered myself an intellectual most of my life. My mind is my weapon. It's sharp and I like to shove it into places.' He chuckles, amused by himself. 'I know what it's like to question. My parents were Protestant Christians, and I didn't believe. Thought it all absolute… horseshit.'

He glances over at me. I count the terraced houses and their square windows.

'And at uni… you know, your parents never got there, but I'm sure you will.' He shunts gears. 'I have no doubt you will… and when I was there, I tried to grab on to a lot of things, you see, time, poetry, language, love, theory.'

He twists the car around a corner, shaking his head, rattling the beads.

'Fucking theory,' he says, laughing at himself. 'These ideas, these constructs all just crumbled. I wanted to be in love, to be honest with you. I couldn't get it. Girls thought I was… they always said I was… too intense.'

I lose count of the windows so pick at the curling fabric on the car door. In his letter, my dad wrote that he is a lodger in a family home, which means that some other family – the wrong family – has him in their house, whereas I am here with Bill.

'When I first saw the Guru's followers, I thought they were idiots,' he says, again looking at me, thinking he is winning me over. 'All smiley.'

'Yeah,' I say.

'You know that smile the leading Premies do? Your mum always calls them Divine Androids, and she's not wrong. But then I received it, Sue, you know, it's impossible to explain. I needed it. It was something other than the mind, the intellectual pursuits, like your books you read all the time. It was something else, I needed it, and when I received the Knowledge I came out feeling wonder. Like I was a kid again. Actual wonder.'

Gemma in my mind: *What are the options? Kill him? Speak to your mum, speak to your dad? Yellow ukelele. Would you like one, Suzy-Sue? Joint from the ashtray. Little square dipped in acid, good for the brain cells.* He yanks on the gearstick and I close my eyes. Silent letters float out of my mouth: D G C Q S D A S D. My fingers twitch, hot under the nails, needing to write. Bill looks at himself in the rear-view mirror.

'It was hard at first. Difficult, even though the secret… techniques are simple, they are hard to do in practice really, meaningfully. But my bigger problem was that I couldn't find a way to connect with Guru himself, you know. In a true, real way.'

I touch the winding handle that pulls the glass window down. In order not to speak or shout at him, I hum lightly as he speaks. More letters make a chain across the windscreen in front of me: L X Q U Q P E S F D F Z.

'But you know what happened?'

'What?' I say, because I sense I'm supposed to.

'Maharaj Ji looked at me. And I knew that I was in the presence of a Superior Power. I knew that I was in awe of him. It didn't take long, a second or so, and it completely turned everything around for me. The intelligence, the thinking, you know, it flipped it around. It was both traumatic and mystical.'

'Okay,' I repeat.

He whispers, 'Ultimate... ruler... Did your dad tell you the same thing? What happened to him?'

I shake my head. Bill is silent for a minute. He's driven a wide circle around the whole estate and is heading back in the direction of our house.

'I don't know if your dad... if he has it in him... your mum, however.'

I cough.

'Your dad is more dedicated though, bless him. Like, he's thirsty, he's ready to believe, but I'm just not sure he's there. Your mum's a brainbox. Questioner and a thinker. Like you.'

Bill has the face of a thief. He carries on talking, but I stop listening apart from the odd word or phrase... *re-adjustment... nothing lives up to the Guru... everything else in life is meaningless... something deep and beautiful happening inside... Don't use the brain, use the heart... alignment. Don't think. Alignment. It's in the body. It's in the breath. Alignment.*

I'm concentrating on steadying my shaking hands and controlling my teeth. His voice has a way of coming into the brain, like the tapes.

'You know, Sue, once you've seen the way, been part of the way, you can never change it. It's an irreversible activity.'

I don't say anything.

'It works in subliminal ways, you see. It takes the bad bits of you, the nasty, cruel, petty, vain, disgusting bits that are inside of you and it makes you look at them, and I mean really look at them. You understand what you are. What lies you've told. What sneaky little jealousies you've had. What a sneak you can be. What a filthy perverted little creepy evil spirit you can be, right, and it brings all of that up to the surface, and then, when you're ready, you let Him in, and you repeat it, you follow it, you say it until you believe it, and then you're free. That's how it works.'

I listen to the car's engine; I try to get my breathing in order.

He is smiling. 'It's like a secret room, a gate that takes you to a private little place, and once you're stripped down, naked in your head, exposed in your brain, I can get you to do anything. I can get your mum and dad to do anything – for Him, of course – like, for example, if they want to leave I will say to them, down in that secret room, you will have to kill yourself before you can leave.'

I put my hands on the steering wheel and twist it hard. The car lurches to the right and rams up the kerb. Bill slams on the brakes and we just miss a lamp post. The beads clatter against the windscreen.

'What the fuck, Sue,' Bill says, as a car coming behind us beeps loudly. 'What was that?'

I am about to cry, but I hide it from him. Why? At my failure? I don't know. If Maharaj Ji is human and not God but is still somehow in charge of everything, what does it mean about this moment? I'm so hot now I can't hear my thoughts.

He pulls up towards our house. I'm desolate with the feeling that I've lost something. He turns off the engine, puts his hand on my wrist and holds it tight. He sniffs. 'Did your dad reveal the Guru's sacred techniques to you, Sue? Before you're ready? Unauthorized?'

There is a shape lurking outside the car. I know it's Mickey before I can even see him properly, something about his shadow. Bill doesn't notice him.

Bill sniffs violently. I wish Gemma were here. She'd poke him in the eyes. Gemma showed me a scar once on the inside of her thigh. She said she got it from falling off a tree, crashing down two, three branches. It was impressive, a bright line. I told her it was like a shark bite. In the car, with Bill's hand on me and Mickey outside peering in like some kind of terrier staring down into a foxhole, I remembered her saying: 'Did you know sharks never sleep?' In return, I'd shared with her my belief in the power of the pencil case. 'What do you mean?' she said, squinting at my WH Smith pencil case. 'It's your own,' I replied. 'It's private. You can control what goes in there. With all the instruments, pens and pencils you can control the world! Don't you see?' And she took out a pen and said, 'I don't think I quite feel the same as you about stationery, you weirdo,' and whacked me on the arm.

Bill shifts in his seat and leans close. 'It's okay, you can tell me.'

I look down at his fingers pressing into my arm. 'You can't lock me in here,' I say.

'Of course not.' There is a violent knock on the window on his side and Bill recoils. He releases my arm. 'Holy shit.' He winds down the window. 'What?'

Mickey looks past Bill to me. 'You all right, Suzanne?' I open the car door and run across the road towards our house. I bang on the front door. My mum opens it and we watch. Mickey and Bill are talking closely, Mickey leaning in nasty and wiry and holding on to the coat collar of Bill's suede hippy jacket. Mickey shoves Bill up against the car and spits in his face.

'What's happening?' my mum said. 'Why is Mickey there?'

I want to fling my arms around you, I think. The words materialize like that: *Fling. Arms. Hold. Mother.* I move towards her and touch her.

Mum is scowling. 'Let's close the door,' I say. I mean: let's banish these men. Let's lock out those two vampires and only let Dad back in, that would be safer. Can't you see that? But she shakes me off. She has a joint in her hand, I notice, and she opens the door wide, wide away-oh.

'Your psychotic little child nearly killed us.' Bill is at the gate behind me. 'And then your even more psychotic neighbour just laid into me for no reason.' He rubs the side of his face, scratches at his beard. The top of my head is so hot now I think it's on fire, and I'm sure there must be sweat in my ears.

I am at the bottom of the stairs, waiting. I think Dave is at the top of the stairs watching. Bill is on the front doorstep now. I move back to the door and try to push it to block him out, to stop him coming in.

Bill jams the door open with his foot. 'Sue, let me in,' he says.

'Sue, what the hell are you doing?' my mum says. I release the door and try to pull on her. She's clingy, she just gets everywhere. This is the wrong life. She is stopping us. 'Best you go, we'll talk about it later,' she says to Bill. She puts her hand on his chest, pushes him out of the door and closes it. She turns to me. 'What's going on?' Her eyes are wild. Her vibrations fill the hall. She floats up from the floor and hovers above me. Her wings span the width of the house, and I cower. Fire comes out of her mouth and nose. We are locked together by a stream of fire. I can't erase her from my existence. She is stuck with me.

'I think they're both vampires,' I say.

'What?' She looks at me.

'They're bad,' I say. 'Can't you see it?'

Mum is sighing now. The wings deflating, the body falling, the feet touching the lino. She squints at me; the wings are gone. She bats my fingers off when I try to hold on. She is tense until finally the vivid energy dissolves. The air around us is flat. 'Why are you shaking? Oh God,' she says, 'you're really shaking. Come on, Sue, let's get you to bed, come on.'

*

At my Irish nana's, I suck down cups of loose-leaf tea and watch the horse racing. On the news, a bogeyman called Gerry Adams makes her swear. We have been bundled here while they move everything out and I've forgotten about my typewriter. 'I need to go back to the house,' I say.

'What for?' She stirs a great saucepan full of dumplings and barley and stewing meat and clumps of garlic and carrots and barely looks around at me. Since my Uncle Gordon's death, she's become more religious, more inclined to snap.

I am agitating near the back door. 'There's something I've forgotten, and I don't want Mum to throw it away.'

'We'll give her a ring then. It's too far and late to walk over now, they'll be finishing up soon and coming here to get you.'

'No phone, Nana.'

She tuts into her stew and glances out of the window. 'What is it?' She looks at me, shrewd through her specs. I know there is no point crying with her. I hold my hands out in helplessness. 'It's going to rain,' she says, 'but go on then. You can take the bike in the shed.'

I guess it's about two miles across Crewe. I cycle through her estate, not fancying the park as the sun is going down. I am out of puff by the time I turn into our road. The house is already different because the curtains are gone. I peep in, and the lines of the room are different with no furniture. I hear a voice calling me. It is Gemma standing with her mum, Mickey and all the other kids. They are bundling bags and stuff.

'Sue,' Gemma shouts. I go over to them. Mickey is filling up the boot with tatty-looking suitcases.

'Where are you going?' I ask.

'Caravan in Prestatyn for a week.' Mickey stands up from shoving suitcases in the boot and looks at me sideways. Gemma is about to say something when her mum comes over, up close, assessing me. She's so short she's only an inch or so taller than me, and it occurs to me that I've never known her name.

'Look after yourself, Suzanne.' Her high voice sounds younger than her face. 'Your parents never really fitted in here, did they?' I look down at my shoes, full of hot shame. 'I always felt you would, though, if you had a different…' She pats her jeans pocket, looking for cigarettes probably, and looks up to the sky for a second. 'A different mother.'

I scrape at the skin on my wrist and blush. 'Okay,' I say, not knowing how to respond.

'Yours is just so… all quiet and sneaky.' She pulls a packet of Marlboro Reds out of her pocket, lights one with a lime-green lighter and smiles at me, though her eyes remain nasty. 'Don't you think, Suzanne? Have you found that about your mum?'

I swallow spit in my mouth. 'What?' I'm confused.

Mickey moves closer. 'You're all packed up then?'

I nod, but Gemma's mum hasn't finished. Gemma is swaying on her feet. Her left hand is in a fist.

'Seen her coming and going, in and out, lifts here and there when your dad was at work, and then of course when he was gone.' She blows out smoke and smiles.

Mickey leans in, smelling of oil and cigarettes. 'What you on about?'

'Suzanne's mum here. Her… shenanigans. I've watched 'em all from the window. Who's your mum in bed with?'

Mickey tuts. 'Give it a rest.' He spits the words at her. 'Where you moving to then?' he says to me.

'Sunny south,' I replied.

'That'll be nice.'

Gemma's mum turns towards him. 'When you been south? Never.' He shrugs. Two of the smaller children start scrapping, nappy and hair, scream and spit. 'Shut up. In the car,' she shouts, bored of me. No interest any more, and no goodbye.

'Your house looks weird empty,' Gemma says, wriggling her backpack on her shoulders.

'Want to come and look in the window together one last time?' I say. We turn together to cross the road.

'Be quick, Gemma. Bye, Suzanne,' Mickey says, giving me a half-smile. 'Have a good life then.' I don't reply. We wait for a bus to pass, and then cross the road and peer in the window. We put our hands on the glass.

'They've got rid of every single thing,' I say, thinking of my diaries, typewriter, all of it. 'I need to tell you something, Gemma,' I said. 'Mickey… he…' She looks me directly in the eye and pushes her palm flat on her nose.

'I know. It's better you're going. He can think about someone else.'

'But you?'

'I can look after myself, don't worry about that.' She bares her teeth like a rat might when trapped. I see there is something on the floor holding the door to the living room open.

'Ah, it's my book,' I say. It's the *Hatha Yoga Pradipika* from the library. In the corner of the room, though I swear it wasn't earlier. So it wasn't lost. Gemma looks in.

'It's locked in now,' I say.

'You want it?' Gemma asks, and I nod. She looks around the front garden and picks up a brick from under an overgrown bay tree. She climbs on the window ledge and bangs the brick into the smallest pane, knocking the glass straight out. She puts in her hand and slides the window up.

'Gemma, come on!' Mickey's voice. 'What you doing?'

She is in and out of the room fast and holds the book towards me. 'God, it's heavy.'

I remember the stones in her bag to hold her steady. 'Is it a good weight to keep you still?'

She opens up her bag, puts it in, tries it on. Her shoulders relax. 'Yeah, actually, that does it.'

'You keep it then,' I say.

Council houses never belong to you. Even if you're part of Thatcher's scheme to buy your own it isn't the same as a house in the woods or at the end of a lane. One of the Premies who visited was a builder, and he told me that houses are made of frames filled with horsehair and spit. On a telegraph wire, I think I see a blue canary.

'All things perish. Everything is fragile, meaningless, I need your love just so I can go on living, wrap me in your love and write your name all over me so I can tell them I belong to you now…'

There is the sound again. I know it without looking round. Individual bricks being poked out, picked out, unstitched, like a loop of embroidery. A tile landing on the pavement next to my feet. A tickle inside my lungs. Not a gremlin. A new thing, an evolved, invasive entity. Winged, flighty and ready to stretch around the world and suffocate everything with its feathers.

WINTER

We have nothing else to know but one thing. Sit in a peaceful place and do meditation. Eat and meditate and listen to satsang. You cannot meditate when on one side the child is calling to you, 'Mother, mother!' So, we should do meditation in a quiet place, away from the child.

'Maharaji's Early Days Satsangs',
Divine Light magazine, special edition, 1966

Council House 2, Late 1980s

Daniella talks about sex all day despite the dispiriting weather. It's as if she's been having it for decades, even though she is only eighteen. I absorb vocabulary and gain specific details with interest. She smokes menthol cigarettes in long slow sucks. She has lazy, Italian-sexy eyes and doesn't care how young and ignorant I am because until I arrive at Bianchi's ice-cream parlour she's had literally, Suzanne, lit-e-ra-lly, no one to talk to.

Seaside towns are the pits. Our new council house has a garden that backs on to the Downs, and this summer holiday job is to stand at the hatch that opens out on to the wild, windy seafront and hand out samples of ice cream to passers-by. I am not allowed to go in the kitchen where Egyptian and Italian men wash up and play card games because at thirteen-about-to-turn-fourteen I am technically too young to work there. I'm paid off the books.

'Where are you from?' Daniella says. 'Your accent is different.'

'Dunno,' I say, not knowing how to articulate Crewe. 'North.' Daniella is the second cousin twice removed from the Bianchi family. She has been exiled here because of 'incidents' at her home in Puglia. On our breaks, we walk Eastbourne's promenade and shout at the disgusting seagulls. 'Puglia is hot and boring,' she says, 'but here it's like a coffin.' Daniella lives in the flat above the cafe and lets me hang out in a room made up of a fold-down bed and a host of inherited mother-in-law's tongue plants. 'In Italian we say *suocera lingua. Impianto.*'

My Irish nana sent me some money for my birthday, so I bought Paul Simon's *Graceland* from Eastbourne's only record shop. I put on the cassette in her flat and lounge on her bed.

When Daniella applies mascara, she peels her eyelid right back to expose the veiny red underside. She makes meatballs with thick red sauce and lengths and lengths of spaghetti. She says the water needs to be as salty as seawater and makes me stick my finger in to test. 'What a baby you are, *piccolo ragazza*,' she says when I confess to not being able to cook anything.

'Have you ever worn fur?' I ask.

'Of course.'

I find a fur coat in a charity shop. Thick. Shaggy. Mothy. Red-grey-brown. I stroke the fur downwards then disturb its flow by running my hand back up. I have been a vegetarian for as long as I can remember. I have rarely eaten meat, apart from the accidental sausage roll at a birthday party or an enforced ham sandwich at a group picnic. I pull out the coat. What kind of animal did it once house? I put my face in the fur.

The woman behind the counter has long, heavy earrings that pull down the holes in her earlobes into lines and eyes that can't be bothered to focus. She says it's from the 1930s and that I look glamorous in it.

'How much is it?'

She slowly puts down her pencil. 'How much have you got?'

My face twitches with hope. I look in my purse. 'Ten pounds.' The woman shakes her head and goes back to her crossword, tutting. I look at myself in the mirror. Wrapped in the animal, I'm different.

'Could you put the coat back on the hanger, please,' the woman says.

'Maybe we could have spaghetti bolognese one time?' I say to Mum as she dumps a can of baked beans in a saucepan.

Daniella wants to meet my family. I take a long look at our house to assess whether I can bring her back. Now we only have one Maharaj Ji picture up. A framed, almost normal-looking photograph of an Indian man in a suit. The lotus flowers and jewels have gone. They still meditate, but they make less of a deal of it. Seem to anyway. Mum's shifts in an old people's home are between nine and fourteen hours, with half-hour breaks. Dad is allowed to bring home the delivery van at weekends.

'Sure,' she says, turning on the gas ring. 'Bolognese, okay, and I'll get caviar too.'

I combine the new school with the Saturday job. I do the bare minimum at school, turning in homework without enthusiasm. The girls are friendly enough. They shunt aggressively around netball courts and have concrete life plans. I prefer Daniella. I put on *Graceland* and sit down to write a letter to her. I write to her most evenings. After our shift, we often go to the pier to see the glass-blower in his shop. He blows through a long pipe into gloopy globs of liquid held over a Bunsen burner. He makes glass poodles, swans and – my favourite – dolphins. I have a notion that I would like to get a dolphin for Daniella's nineteenth birthday, which is coming up apparently, but it is £25.

'We're having satsang tonight, so will need you in bed in Dave's room by 7.30, okay?'

It's the first time they've used that word in Eastbourne. 'What?'

'You heard.' Mum moves quickly through the room, picking up socks, cardigans.

'That's way too early. I can't go to bed then.'

Her eyes flick across the room towards me. 'Not now,' she says.

I pinch the skin on my wrist in frustration. 'Mum, can I have twenty-five pounds when you next get paid?'

'What for?'

'A glass dolphin.'

She shakes her head. 'I don't have spare cash, you know that, not for things like that…'

I don't go downstairs later, but I hear voices in the living room, see them coming in the front door. New satsang people. Laughter. Incense. Dave is on his bed reading *Asterix*. I stay there with him for a while and wish I could read graphic novels or comics, but I seem to be stuck in a universe of words. I work hard to rearrange the vowels in my mouth, standing in front of the mirror: *caaa-stle. Baa-thh.* I am full of shame about Crewe. Then ashamed of the shame.

Daniella wants me to go with her to Brighton. Elton John is opening a new Aids ward at the hospital. I want to go, though I am afraid of Aids and the adverts on the TV. USE CONDOMS! BE SAFE! AIDS KILLS!!! I'm not allowed as Mum has a shift.

Dave, Dad and I walk slowly to the pier. Half-term, the weather filthy and the seafront empty. The Bianchis have 'let me go' until the season starts up again in Easter. It seems a long time away. The sea looks bleak and broken under the weight of the rain. The 'sunny south'? When I think of Crewe, I can't tell which part of my life is a memory and which is happening now.

Holding up my anorak hoods, I lead Dad to the glass-blower's shop. We watch him conjuring up an octopus with his glassy spins of green and blue. I lean into my dad, missing something, remembering something, though not sure what. The thought of Gemma on her bike comes through my mind. I push it away.

'I like the dolphin.' Dad squints in at the price tag.

'You do?'

'Yeah.' He buys it for me, and a tiny glass dog for Dave. The glass-blower tells us he's shutting up tomorrow, for the winter season.

I am getting back from walking a neighbour's dog with Dave when I notice the brown Thunderbird parked in front of our house. 'Is that Bill's?'

Dave looks up from scuffing gravel on the edge of the kerb. 'Yeah,' he says, sniffing.

The car door swings open, and we see him getting out. Long suede jacket, but not his trademark Stetson. He turns and sees us, 'Hello sailors,' he says. 'Who's the mutt?'

'I have to take him back to his owners,' I say, pulling the dog away and walking towards the neighbour's gate. Dave stays back with me. We watch Bill go through the front door of our house. We hang around outside, avoiding going in until we can wait no longer.

'I need the loo,' Dave says.

'Yeah.'

Inside the house, shoulders hunched up, humming and smoking a joint, my dad is stirring something gloopy in a saucepan. 'Lentil stew,' he says.

Since being here we have not had a single lentil. Or bean. Or fermented anything. Nor a medjool date or a chickpea. Nor marijuana. We've been living on fish finger wraps, Heinz beans, baked potatoes, mashed potatoes, chips and peas. Dave and my mum have even been eating Bernard Matthews chicken goujons. Bernard Matthews chicken Kievs. On the table is a sealed jar of home-made something with floating butter beans. The entire house already smells of Bill. 'I don't like lentil stew,' I say.

'Since when?'

'Since always.'

'Well, I've witnessed you eating it many times.' He smiles, stirring the gloop.

'Yeah, well, I never liked it.'

Bill's rumbling voice comes from the living room, and I hear Dave and Mum laughing. I put my hand against the wall and then run up to my room. Bill's carpetbag with the leather tassels hanging off the zip is on my bed. His sandals are tucked underneath.

I run back downstairs. 'Why is Bill's bag on my bed?'

'He's staying for a little while.'

I concentrate my eyes on the hedge at the bottom of the garden. I think of the unbelievable softness of the neighbour's dog's ears and how when I walk him on the Downs he becomes alert and focused when another person walks towards me. 'Why?'

'Well...' My dad examines his half-smoked joint and relights it on the gas ring. He puffs it into the lentil stew. 'Carys has kicked him out.' Carys of the marmalade hair. 'Harmony's pregnant, and he went crazy and it all went horribly, horribly wrong, and now he's here.'

'Oh?'

'He deserves to be kicked out, I'm sure.' My dad winks. 'But he's done so much for us, you know, I want to give something back.'

'Yeah,' I say. 'But why is his bag in my room?'

Mum walks in at this point and leans against the door frame. Ignoring me, she looks at Dad. 'It's really bad.' She shakes her head.

'He's not having my room,' I say. Neither of them respond. 'I mean it. He can't have it. How long is he here for?'

'Just till he gets sorted.'

'What does that mean? Why can't he have Dave's room?'

212 · THE MUSEUM OF LOST AND FRAGILE THINGS

'Because the ley line crosses at a complex angle and Bill
can't sleep in there,' my mum says. I think she's being sarcastic
until I realize she isn't.

'But the ley lines are okay in my bigger, sunnier room?'
I say, and my dad laughs. 'Is Harmony going to have a
baby?'

'Yep, at home, with Carys, and they don't want Bill
around.' I remember Carys's pantry room and comforting
atmosphere. If I were to have a baby, I'd have it in there. I
wouldn't want Bill either. 'Just a couple of weeks,' she says.
'You can bunk in with Dave.'

'I hate you both.'

In the living room Bill is balancing a picture of Maharaj
Ji on the mantelpiece. 'What do you think, Sue?' he says.
'In the middle, or further to the left?'

I slam the door and run upstairs. The landing has shrunk,
the bathroom has shrunk. When we first moved into the
council house swap, the rooms felt bigger. Now there is no
room to think. Life, then, is a game that always ends up with
me back in the same place.

Bill is standing at the bottom of the stairs. 'Sue,' he shouts,
and waves something at me. 'Look, a CD! No more crappy
tapes.' He comes up behind me and goes into my room. He
has already plugged in a small portable CD player. He turns
it on, grinning at me.

*Enjoy. Enjoy what you have because it's yours and nobody
can take it away from you. This is one thing that you will always
have, and this is one thing that you will have till the day you die.
It's all yours. Is God-given, nature-given, whatever you believe*

*in, it's given to you. I want to thank you, thank you for hearing
me out, for what I have to...*

Then he comes out of the room and lopes down the stairs
again. I hear him say to Dad, 'Well, late spring, next year.
That's when they're running the part-time instructors' course
in Brighton. Until then...'

When I brush my teeth, I see that Bill uses a charcoal-
eucalyptus salt mix that has made the bathtub go black.

'Where do you go when you walk that dog?' Bill says.
'Can I come with you?'

'No.'

He gives me a surprised look.

'Are you still a vegetarian, Bill?' I ask.

'Of course,' he says.

Daniella is full of how exciting it was in Brighton. The Aids
victims were noble and magnificent. Elton John brushed past
her, was gracious to everyone and wore his trademark glasses.

'Elton's *Reg Strikes Back* is a work of genius,' Daniella
says. I lean against the door of her flat, holding the blue glass
dolphin. She bobs her head to Elton's 'I Don't Wanna Go
On with You Like That'.

'Got this for you.'

She takes it and holds up the dolphin appreciatively. In
the window light, the swirls of blue and white are like clouds
trapped inside the glass. 'It's nice,' she says in her Italian
sing-song voice. 'Thanks.' Then she sighs and flops on the
floor. 'Going to Brighton has made me think.'

'Oh?'

'I hate it here, I do. This shit town. Look at the sky. I hate working for my auntie, she's such a beetch.' I nod in agreement at that. 'And you… at school. You're just a little…'

'What?'

Daniella gestures to the window. 'Teeny weeny schoolgirl. Sucked into the system. Crunched into it, yeh.'

My chin drops to my chest. I'm deflated. I'd imagined, somehow, that our friendship transcended my age.

'I'm going to London,' she says, sitting up. 'I've decided. On Monday. I'm getting a National Express coach.'

'You're leaving?' It's hard to control my voice.

'I have a friend from Italy, and he told me of a place where I can stay, where we can stay.'

'We can stay?'

'Yes, you can come if you like.' She says it casually, as if offering me sugar in my tea.

'London?'

'Yes.'

London. I've been twice. Once to the West End, for a performance of *Cats*. Another time to the Tower of London with school. Herded from one place to another, frogmarched into a coach and not allowed to use the toilet for hours. I remembered the grey river, stinky air and black cabs. 'What is it, the place?'

'A big shared house… a… what's the word? I can't think of the word… trying to think of the word…'

'What?'

'A squat,' she says, smiling, with her dimples and her clumpy mascara. 'Think about it,' she says. 'Monday.'

I take the dolphin back when she is in the bathroom. I'm sure she won't even notice.

The phone rings. It's Carys. Dave and I listen to Bill slamming his hand against the wall and swearing.

'You're stuck between a rock and a hard place if you have kids,' he says when he's done. 'You have to wait until they're grown up and out of your hair so that you can surrender yourself fully, or you have to dump them somewhere.'

The phone immediately rings again. 'What does she want?' Dad says.

'She wants money, otherwise she's going to lose the house.' Bill is scowling.

I think of Harmony's geodome at the bottom of the garden, of the rambling garden of that house. All washing away into a great big sea of drained money flowing out through an ocean of Knowledge, piling up on the shore of Malibu, spilling piles of gold on to Maharaj Ji's private beach. What does it mean to lose a house? A mislaid house, put down on the carpet or left in the post office like a pair of glasses? To lose a house implies that it is accidentally misplaced, an annoyance. What do I know about anything? Nothing. But I am pleased that Mum doesn't seem to like Bill any more. It seems she might even be unsure about Maharaj Ji.

Seeing as it is in my room, I rummage through Bill's stuff. I quickly discover his stash in his shoe under the bed. £120. I steal £20 and go quickly back to the charity shop.

'It's thirty pounds,' the woman says. Radio 4 is on. A bluebottle lands on the till for a second then buzzes off. I look around as if to say, well, there aren't many other customers in here. 'Oh, all right,' she says, capitulating and sighing.

I step out into the streets of Eastbourne wearing the fur coat. I wander for a bit, then go to Camilla's bookshop until the owner gets fed up with me reading and not buying anything. Finally, I slope home.

The kitchen table is covered with papers. Bill is hunched over them, waving a pair of scissors, chewing something. Liquorice. He loves it. The smell makes me want to gag.

'What's happening?'

'We're giving service,' Bill says. 'Working on the materials for the Festival of Knowledge.'

I look out of the window. Mum is in the garden, smoking a cigarette and looking up at the sky. I go out to her, and she barely acknowledges me. 'Do you still believe all this stuff, Mum?' I say.

She jumps. 'Sue, Jesus, I didn't know you were there.' She is upset and has been crying. 'What?'

'Why is all the Maharaj Ji stuff still here again?'

She makes a weird little noise. 'What happened to you, Sue? I thought you had your special relationship with Maharaj Ji.'

I stand up straight. I am about to launch into a complaint about Bill. In our house, in my room. It occurs to me that she's quoting me directly from my diary. There is something odd about her face and I realize she's in war mode. The trees in my lungs contract. She is a verbal fighter, her weapons are words, and she has stolen mine to use against me.

'You and Dad, sharing the techniques, meditating together. Private little moments.' She is very sarcastic.

'You've been reading my—'

'Lost your faith, Suzy-Sue?' She is sneering. She sucks deeply on her cigarette; her hands are shaking.

'I think it's a violation of my privacy to read what I—'

'How did I create such a sanctimonious, judgemental person?'

She is smiling, but it is a nasty smile. I can never see her properly. Either everything feels too wide and we are far apart, or I am too close to focus.

'When I received the Knowledge,' she says, throwing her cigarette on the grass, 'we went to Manchester with Premie friends and had to wait outside the hall. The traffic was terrifying. I couldn't get across the road. A policeman shouted at me because I was in the way and a bus was coming and I couldn't move.'

I don't say anything. I'm tense and ready for anything.

'I wanted the bus to take me,' she says. Her eyes are searching my face, analysing my reaction. She wants a response. I don't know what she means. I feel like she is feeding on me, wanting to absorb and suck in emotions.

'Take me?' I say.

'I wanted the bus to run me over,' she says in a flat, cold voice.

I have no idea what to say. I am thirteen. I don't have any words. In a nearby garden, kids are playing football. There is a screech as one player kicks another. A dog somewhere close lets out a few quick yaps.

'When I received the Knowledge,' she repeats, 'I lost my scarf.' She says this as if it is super-meaningful and significant. 'You and Dad and your secret little meetings,' she repeats. I think she is going to say that now she doesn't believe, that Maharaj Ji and Bill and the whole Divine Light business is rubbish, but she turns and looks at me. 'Everything is meaningless without it.'

'The scarf?'

'No, the belief. But in some senses I can't go further with it. To the places Bill and your dad want to go. So, you see, I'm lost in the middle, though at least they have you.'

All I want, I think, is a mum who'll give me some biscuits or a sandwich and a drink when I get home from school and not be weird about scarves and stare intensely up at the sky like this.

Also, I want my room back.

Tonight, a satsang. The familiar smell of incense in the house, and Maharaj Ji's portrait looms over a potpourri bowl with curled-up petals that look like fingernails. There are about six people. One is a smiley-looking farmer called Jeremy. He comes into the kitchen and puts down a crate of apples. He holds one up in front of my face. 'Know what this is?'

'Apple,' I say, rolling my eyes. Fucking hippies.

'Pinova,' he says. 'And this?' Another one, greener. 'This is Elstar. Try it. They are from my orchard.' I take it from him and go upstairs.

'They're back,' I say. Dave shrugs. I am jealous of his ability to zone out completely, not to be bothered. I am sick of being in his room, with his *Star Wars* figures and his half-drunk glasses of milk everywhere. I look at him. 'What's that on your skin?' He turns away from me, but I grab his arm. It is covered in scabby, dry skin. I go to my old room feeling shitty and responsible.

I pick up the backpack that was bought 'at great expense' for school. I creep down to the kitchen and fill it with twenty apples from the crate Jeremy brought with him. I slip my hand in Mum's purse and steal what money's in there.

Bill coughs. He's behind me, but I don't think he saw me with the purse. 'Is that real fur?' he says, pointing at my coat.

I pull it closer around me. 'Yeah.'

He screws up his nose. 'Doesn't it make you feel weird wearing it?'

I don't answer. When he's gone, I go up the stairs and look in the full-length mirror on the back of the bathroom door. How does the coat make me feel? I run my hands over it.

The animal, whatever it was, speaks to me. 'You're out of here,' it says. 'Out of the present tense of your childhood.'

'Where to?' I ask it.

But there's no reply.

Beachy Head

She drops to her knees in the grass about a metre from the edge of the cliff. The sky around us is unreal, like a painting. We are at the local beauty spot, Beachy Head.

In parts the grass sinks in clumps and dips, and it's hard to see where the land ends. In other areas, the rim is clear, the sense of an agitated sea beyond. I haven't noticed her yet. I'm looking at the wide horizon and seagulls like coat hangers in the sky. Wild and windy so our heads are blown off. Dad and Dave up ahead. The world is empty apart from us. Our little insignificant family.

I dawdle, trying to understand chalk. Is it made of bone? Crushed skeletons? It's so different from the claggy orange-brown soil in Cheshire. You get a whoosh of vertigo if you get too close to the edge.

The colours and wind up here don't quite make sense but are powerful. I am new and refreshed. I am possibility. Thinking about a future, wide as sky. I can be a writer. Or an artist? The author of *The Family from One End Street* did both. I'm deliberating between these two. I like ink, marks, pages and tents made by books upended. Can I be both?

Before we moved here, Dad told me about Beachy Head in a letter and how articles in the local paper said it happens weekly. Locals call them jumpers, slippers, fallers or fliers. I look round to see if anyone is lurking on the edge and then I see Mum, on the floor. She's on her knees, scraping her hands into the grassy chalk land like dogs do when they are trying to get through the wiring of the fence, to chase a rat or to escape. 'Mum? Did you fall over?' I run along the path towards her.

Mum has flattened herself on the floor, and when she looks up I can see that she's crying. I shout for Dad, Bill and Dave, but they are too far ahead, looking the other way.

I crouch. 'Mum, what's happening?' She is mumbling, and I strain to understand. 'Get me away from the edge,' she's whispering.

Finally, Dad turns around. He rushes over, and we pull her away. There's a bench close by. 'Don't look at it,' Dad says. 'Don't look at the sky out there.'

'Are you okay, Mum?' Dave says.

Dad holds her very tight, very close. 'It's okay. Look away. It's okay.'

Squat, Early 1990s

Daniella and I sat at the back, and I taught her the words to 'He Jumped Without a Parachute'. The coach was mostly empty apart from some tourist families at the front. Sussex quickly turned into nowhere land, then motorway, then the concrete edges of London, and then London proper.

The money I'd stolen came to £43 thanks to an additional £30 found in Bill's cords. I'd used a third of it to buy the coach ticket. I had some clothes, books, but beyond that I had nothing. At the top of a road leading through Streatham, I saw a sign saying LITTLE MOROCCO and peered down a street of cafes with dainty chairs outside and dark windows. When the coach pulled up at Victoria Coach Station, belching out its pollution, I grabbed my bag and hopped on to the concrete. I followed Daniella obediently. She had an A–Z and we puzzled over the grid and the way page thirty-five became page eighty-six.

Finally, we found the address. It was a tall terrace on Earl's Court Gardens near the Tube. Steps led up to a faded blue front door, and inside the place was huge, draughty and falling apart. Two tall Italian men stood at the door smiling at us.

On the ground floor, the large front room was run by a guy in an anti-fascist punk band. Most of the rooms on the first and second floors were taken by a range of Italian drifters. The top floor was full of New Zealanders and Australians. They spoke to Daniella in a rush and showed us a room that had graffiti on the walls and somebody's cut toenails embedded into the tufts of what had once presumably been an expensive carpet.

Daniella turned to me. 'Shall we go with them? He works at a restaurant and can get us some dinner.'

But I didn't want to. I was exhausted. I had a headache. I had a packet of red Walkers crisps in my bag, and I wanted to eat them quickly and find somewhere to use the loo. I shook my head. 'I'm going to stay here,' I said.

One of the Italian men was looking at me. 'How old are you?' he asked in a strong accent.

'Seventeen.' He raised his eyebrows and assessed my body. I glanced down at myself. I barely had breasts. I put my toes together and held my breath, but he was already saying something else to Daniella.

'You sure you won't come?' Daniella said, but before I'd even confirmed, she was running down the corridor behind the men, laughing.

I sat in the room on one of the two single beds and ate the crisps and apple. The mattress had no sheets and was a grey colour. Luckily, I'd brought a sleeping bag with me. The window looked out over an overground bit of the Tube line. The wallpaper had been fancy once, I could tell. I recognized the print from stationery I'd bought from WH Smith: William

Morris, Strawberry Thief. There was a built-in wardrobe with one of the doors hanging off and inside a lonely coat hanger. I realized I'd forgotten to bring the fur coat. The entire room rumbled with the force of a passing train and then another straight after it. Someone was playing an electric guitar somewhere. There was a screech. A door slamming. Boots running up- and downstairs and someone shouting, 'Callie, fucking come on!' in an Australian accent.

I looked at the sky outside. The sun was going down, and I was starving. I didn't have a watch, but I thought I'd better go and find something else to eat. I went slowly down the stairs and wondered if I should say I was sixteen. Maybe seventeen was pushing it.

When I got to the bottom step a door opened. A man stepped out. He had white make-up on his face, and his eyeliner was drawn so that it looked like he was crying black tears. Half his head was shaved and the other half had dreadlocks. He was extremely tall. I tried to sidle past him, but he blocked me. 'Who are you?' he said.

'Suzanne.'

'What are you doing here?'

'I'm here with… Daniella.' He frowned down at me. 'She's Italian. And some Italian men…'

A woman emerged behind him wearing a full bridal outfit that had been covered in red paint and slashed. Her eyes were so heavily made up that that she looked as though she were dressed for Halloween, though it was the wrong time of year. 'I don't know who that is. What room are you in?'

'The small back one, up there.'

The bloody bride leaned forward and looked at me closely. 'How old are you?'

'Sixteen.'

Two more women came in through the front door, dressed similarly, all breasts, lipstick, eyeliner, boots, matted hair and a combined, strong skunk smell.

The bridal woman shook her head. 'Trouble, Gaz, too young.'

He shrugged and pushed her hand off his arm. 'Twenty quid a week. I'll get it off you later, got a gig now.' Then one of the women, not the bridal one, took his face and gave him a deep kiss. I'd never seen anyone kiss before. He hovered at the door as the women carried black boxes and tangles of guitar leads behind him. They dropped a flyer on the floor, and the door slammed after them. I picked it up. SUPPORT THE ANTI-NAZI LEAGUE GIG £4.00 HOPE & ANCHOR 7 P.M.

Then the huge London house was silent, and I was left staring at the pile of post on the floor. I realized that I didn't have a key, so if I went out I might be stuck. I wished I'd gone out with Daniella and the Italians, but I hadn't wanted to confess something: I'd never eaten in a restaurant. I roamed around the building, creeping as quietly as I could. The kitchen had some kind of infestation, woodlice possibly. There was a bathroom right off the kitchen, but I was too nervous to use the toilet. I could sense other people in the house, but no one came out. I ran back up to the room. I sat alone in there and waited for Daniella.

She didn't come. I was an idiot not to have brought a watch with me. I got changed and went down to the front door. I left the latch up, pulled the door to and went out into my first London night.

Earl's Court Road was as busy – busier, probably – than Eastbourne or Crewe's high street in the middle of a Saturday rush hour, even though it was night-time. I bought a sausage roll and some orange juice and slowly walked until I found a telephone box. I rang home.

Dad picked up. 'Where are you?' I told him. His voice was serious, almost cold. 'Just give me the address, now.' I told him. He made me repeat it three times. 'Who are you there with?' I told him. 'I'm coming now,' he said.

I cringed. 'No, no. Dad. No way, you can't.'

'I don't care, I'm coming.'

'Please. No. I'll just move if you do. I'll go to another place and I won't tell you where I am.'

I could hear his breath. 'Tomorrow, then? Sue?'

I paused. I almost said yes. *Yes, Dad, yes, come tomorrow and get me.* Then I heard my mum's voice in the background. It was rising high. 'What is she doing? London? What?' I heard Bill's voice mingled in. 'No,' I said, 'don't come. Don't come. I'll call you again soon, I promise. If you come here, I'll just leave again.' Dad was saying something, but I couldn't hear. Then the beeps went. I had no more change. I held the telephone receiver next to my nose and wished I'd told my dad to come and get me now.

The receiver smelled of other people's bacteria and spit. I looked at the cards pinned up all over the inside of the telephone box. LUCY WANTS YOU NOW. Girls in bikinis sitting cross-legged with the number to call across their nipples. Girls stretching or leaning over things. Girls with uncomfortable-looking G-string knickers right up their bums, looking back over their shoulders at the camera. ARABIC QUEEN TITTY. LEGGY BLONDE 5′11″. BLACK, EXCITING AND GORGEOUS. VOLUPTUOUS ENGLISH BLONDE. MISTRESS JENNIFER. AFRICAN QUEEN. STUNNING SPANISH GIRL AVAILABLE NOW.

I saw Daniella and the two Italian men coming down the street. I stepped out of the phone box. 'Hey!' the tall one shouted, and he put his arm through mine. He smelled of wine, and I let them drag me along and tell me their stories, half in English and half in Italian.

I spent the next two days reading books that I'd got from the charity shop on the corner and walking up and down Earl's Court Road, trying to find a job. I had bumped into Gaz and his Gothic brides two more times, and each time he'd demanded £20. I'd told him I'd have it by the end of Saturday. Daniella was unable to help now; she was barely in the room. I didn't know where she had gone or what she was doing. She spoke almost exclusively in Italian and sometimes acted as if she didn't even know me.

Although I went into every cafe and every hotel, they all shook their heads and said I was too young. The owner of a cafe called Bokado weighed me up and told me to come back on Saturday if I wanted to trial 'washing-up', and so finally I had a life plan. I just needed to eke out my money until then. I would have to live on sausage rolls, orange juice and crisps from the corner shop.

When I got back from walking along Earl's Court Road the following day there was a note from my parents on the front door. Written in large capital letters, it told me that they were round the corner in the car and would be on the steps at 3 p.m. and again at 5 p.m. They had signed it *John and Lynda*.

I walked to the edge of the road and saw the VW Beetle parked up and shapes of heads inside. I quickly turned around and walked away. I went through the innocuous door of Brompton Library and asked for a copy of the *Hatha Yoga Pradipika*. The librarian was a man who wrote the reference number on a Post-it note and handed it over without looking at me.

It was raining. My dad's VW Beetle would be getting wet. It's always cosy inside a car with rain outside. I located the book and found a corner desk away from anyone else. I immediately felt better being surrounded by books. The student of hatha yoga should practise in a solitary place, in a temple or a hermitage, an arrow shot away from rocks, water and fire. This book was different from the one I'd looked at in Crewe. This had a commentary.

Here we have the first great problem, larger perhaps than that of the siddhis: to find a quiet spot, undisturbed and safe. Predatory animals, earthquakes, and floods: those were the problems at that time. Today's problems are professional, financial, political, which constantly drag the practitioner back into the stream of social life. However, it is not entirely impossible to create a hermitage under modern conditions. Perhaps there is a quiet attic, away from the attractions of movies, radio, television, where we can meet our neglected and ignored own selves.

Reading helped, but I realized my hands were shaking. There was a musky smell. I glanced around, wondering if I'd trodden in something, then realized it was me. I was too frightened to use the bathroom for long. There was no lock, and there was no way I was going to get in the bath. There was no electricity in the squat, but oddly there was hot water.

I looked at a newspaper on the table in front of me. It was 1 September, and the headline said BACK-TO-SCHOOL BLUES. School. It was supposed to be starting in a couple of days. I looked at the clock: 3 p.m. Were my parents still sitting out there? Were they praying to Maharaj Ji? Were they swearing, hating me, scared, angry? I could just stand up now, and walk around to them, and get in the car and return to Eastbourne and school.

But then I thought of Bill and his CD player; of my mum, grinding her cigarette into the grass.

Finding a pencil, I wrote on the margin of the newspaper a list of everything about school: pencil cases, maths, grammar lists, playground traumas, hockey in the rain, badminton in the gym courts, loneliness on the school walk, melancholia in the stairwell, the exhaustion of the teachers, the pettiness of the bullies, the sadness of the dinner ladies, the gravy on the chips, the prison-like nature of the rails, the relief at the end of the day, the tedium at the thought of years and years of it; the comfort at the thought of years and years of it. The horrible Eastbourne girls who had lived there forever and didn't have northern accents.

I started to cry, and I couldn't stop. I thought I would use the techniques to help; I had abandoned them of late.

My 'relationship with Maharaj Ji', as my mum had noted, was confusing. I pushed my fingers against my eyeballs. I counted. I opened up my diaphragm. I breathed. A woman came towards me in a bright blue raincoat. She opened her mouth as if she were about to speak. I looked up, grateful for contact, but saw her right eye blink. There was something off about her make-up. She made a weird clicking noise with her mouth. 'Give me the paper, give me the paper, give me the paper,' she said, her voice rising. I handed it to her. Then I stood up, got out of the library, and ran. It was 5.45; the shops were shutting up. I reached the steps of the house and there was another note from my parents, telling me they would stay until 7 p.m. before going to pick up Dave. They asked me to call them, and told me they were sorry. I hid in my room until 7 p.m. had passed.

I didn't call them for five days. My dad told me later that neither of them could eat properly the whole time I was away; they lived on cigarettes and worry. He came up on his own on the Saturday and left another note, but someone in the squat must have pulled it down before I saw it. Daniella left me a note on the bed one day, saying that she was moving on and wished me good luck. She gave me no more explanation or information, but she must have felt slightly guilty because underneath the note was £10.

I sat alone in the room and read some new books, purchased with my rapidly diminishing resources. Jeanette Winterson. Lucy Ellmann. Toni Morrison's *Jazz*. All women. Too old for me; voraciously swallowed for that reason.

People of the house knocked on my door now. There were some Aussies from upstairs. They were curious, not unfriendly, and after a moment of looking at my face always asked my age.

After I spoke to them, I told them that no, I didn't have any money. Or no, I didn't want to go out into the street with them or go anywhere or do anything. I retreated into my room. I developed a system of wedging the one chair in the room against the handle to stop anyone from being able to burst in.

Sometimes there was a queue of women taking up the entire length of the hall, leading into Gaz's room. They were always dressed up and carried his stuff for him. They seemed to share him and compete to look after him. They gave me hard, cold stares. I mostly came and went unnoticed until one afternoon I bumped into him on the doorstep. He was wearing full make-up. He caught my wrist and flicked me against the wall. My heel banged into the grubby skirting.

'Money.'

'Yes.'

'Now.'

'I don't… I don't…'

Then he looked at me, touched my hair for one second. 'Where are you from?' he said, and then, 'I don't even know your name.'

'Suzanne. Eastbourne.'

He squinted at me. 'You're kidding,' he said. 'Me too! From the dead people on the south coast to the punk revolution.' He laughed.

The woman who had been dressed as a bride appeared and pushed Gaz aside. 'Babe,' she said, 'shouldn't you be at school?' I shook my head and stared at the floor.

'She's from Eastbourne. Can you believe it? But I need that money. I mean it, I don't care how fucking baby-young you are, I run this place.'

The woman took my hand. 'You really should get out of here,' she said, and I didn't think it was unkind.

That night, a person who was high on something walked into the squat and then came into different rooms, slamming doors open and smashing things. Someone shouted, 'Don't approach him.' He had an accent I didn't understand and was stripped to the waist, wearing shorts. He stood at the door to my room, shouting, 'I can't get no satisfaction,' and pulled off his shorts so he was naked. I flattened myself against the window ledge. He looked at me, but I couldn't tell if he could see me. There seemed to be frothy dribble coming from his mouth. He backed out of my room and concentrated his energies on smashing up the bannisters. He was strong enough to pull out each wooden segment.

When everything was quiet again, I poked my head out. There were bits of wood and stains on the carpet, which, now I came to look at it, was filthy.

A voice came from the top of the stairs above me. 'Hey, come here.' It was a girl with long, flat hair curtaining either side. She was Australian and extremely skinny. I walked towards her. She smiled, but her eyes were weird. 'So glad the storm's over. He's gone, I think. I don't like crack.' She spent a moment touching my face and my lips, singing in a low voice. I didn't know how old she was, maybe nineteen, something like that. She was wearing a flowery dress that had the sleeves cut off and was barefoot. 'Have you been up to wonderland?' she asked. I shook my head. She smiled. 'Come on then.'

I followed her up two more flights of stairs, up into the loft area. Voices called out to her from rooms, people sitting on the floor looking over some papers and a person carrying a mug of something. My stomach gave a jerk when I saw the mug, and I realized I was starving. I was so hungry all the time that I felt as if I was moving upwards off the floor. As if my private relationship with gravity had changed and I was no longer locked down in my own body.

'I'm Samantha,' the girl said in her Australian voice, and then she beckoned me into the attic area. There was a bead curtain and then some other fabric hanging down, and a strong smell of synthetic roses.

This area of the house had a different feel from the rest. There were no anti-Nazi punk pictures here as there were downstairs. Instead, there were posters of Indian saints, and I recognized the smell of nag champa mixed with joints. It was a familiar environment, and I relaxed a little.

In the corner of Samantha's room was a little shrine with candles and flowers and in the middle a little pink lotus flower with a goddess holding a baby in it. Samantha smiled when she saw me examining it. 'That's Shashti,' she said, the word bringing out her accent. 'She is the protector of children.'

'Oh,' I said. She smiled and sat cross-legged in front of him. 'How old are you,' she said, 'speaking of children?'

'Fifteen.'

She nodded. 'It's a shit age, but it gets better.'

I glanced around, half expecting to see a picture of Maharaj Ji. 'Have you heard of Guru Maharaj Ji?' I said, trying to be nonchalant and older than I was.

Samantha looked interested. 'No, I haven't, is that your guru? Cool. I'm not surprised, you look wiser than your years. You're young, but you look like you've seen a lot, you know.'

I was pleased with this, and I was surprised. For the first time, mentioning the Guru made me feel welcome rather than freaky. I sat cross-legged.

'Mushroom tea?' she said, pointing to a teapot. I didn't know what that was, so I shook my head. She shrugged.

'I'll teach you some secret ancient techniques if you like,' I said.

She clapped her hands and tucked her long brown hair behind her ears. 'Cool. Who are you? A little magical saint miracle worker? I woke up this morning and spoke to Shashti there and said, I need some help with the spiritual side of things and now you've turned up. That's Shashti for you.' She blew a kiss to her baby-clutching goddess. 'So, what are these techniques? Wait...' She poured me tea from the teapot into a little brown cup. It tasted of mould. 'Had this before?' I shook my head. We sipped, then swallowed. It was gross. 'It's classic, with a little extra.' I didn't know what she meant. 'Go on then,' she said, taking my hand and squeezing it. I showed Samantha how to do the eye pressing and the finger-in-the-ear technique, the secret *kriyas*. She was extremely game and tried them all. Then I told her about the tongue one, and how you had to cut the frenulum at the bottom to reach the third eye. 'Wow,' she kept saying over and over. 'That's so cool.'

I drank more of the tea, even though it was unpleasant, and then I realized: it was 'mushroom tea'. I didn't notice much, perhaps a cramping in my stomach, but after a while the quality of my thoughts did change a little. They became intense as I explained about the third eye and the nectar and looked at Samantha's friendly face in front of me, smiling, nodding and responding. I was enjoying myself, but then I began a counter-narrative in which we weren't in a room but in a car and we were driving around country lanes.

'Are we in a car?' I asked Samantha. She glanced around; she was still trying to get her tongue to touch her forehead to reach her third eye, so couldn't speak. She just nodded.

'We are?' I felt a panic in my chest.

'No, no, I don't think so. This isn't a car.'

I picked up her nag champa box. 'I fucking hate the smell of nag champa,' I said.

She laughed. 'It seems an odd thing to have strong feelings about.'

Samantha was telling me why she was in London. She'd seen a documentary about dogs who work with visually impaired people, and she wanted to train them. Or at least be an animal handler of some description, and I was interested, but I kept having strange visions, quick flashes, intense, and inside my eyelids. I saw pictures in a dome as if it were reaching across the whole world, above me. NO TO THE BLOODY WAR. STOP THE SLAUGHTER. And small Vietnamese children's faces were blown apart, smashed with napalm, destroyed with blood. Then my mum's face, rising above me. Then nasty little revelatory thoughts that on some core level she was shaky, unsafe. Then images of the Guru, early ones when he still wore garlands of flowers.

'I think it would be a good thing to handle wild animals, you know, but cute ones, like hedgehogs and that sort of thing,' Samantha was saying.

Am I like that? I thought. Unsafe. Shaky in the core? I was distracted, momentarily, by the rumbling of the Tube.

Samantha got up and left the room. She came back with a pink Swiss army knife. 'Shall I cut it?' she said.

'What?'

'The fre... fre... fenulummy thing you told me about?'

I looked up. She was pretty in her flowers and her long hair and she was the smiliest, most trustworthy and open person I had ever met, and I wanted to give her my glass dolphin. 'What?' I said.

'To free your tongue from the sins of the mother so that you can be free and put your tongue on your third eye and reach the cosmic universe, like you just said.' Samantha stuck out her tongue and wiggled it at me. She laughed.

I picked up her Moroccan lamp and held it in front of my eyes. This was the thing I had been trying to get to the bottom of. You can't outrun it. You can run along a National Express coach line until you get as far from Eastbourne as you can (London), but it still doesn't get you back to where you used to be (Crewe, that place, but it wasn't a place I was trying to get back to, it was the atmosphere of the place). I said it aloud: 'It was safe there, or at least I wanted it to be.'

'Ah,' said Samantha, as if she knew what I was talking about. She rubbed her chin, pretending it was a beard, being an intellectual, being a serious thinker, 'Where are we girls safe?'

'Yes, where?'

'Not where my uncle or my cousins are, I can tell you that,' she said.

I opened my mouth. 'Go on then.'

'What?' Samantha was running her hand over her neck. 'Fren... ul... um.'

She sprang up, remembering. 'Oh yes.' She looked excited and she took off her dress so she was just in a pair of knickers, and examined the pink knife closely.

Aside from my mum's breasts and some sagging huge ones on the women rubbing towels vigorously on the heads of their kids in the swimming baths, I hadn't seen any bare-chested women. Samantha was skinny, with ribs and spine sticking out. She was twisty and moved a bit like a snake. Her breasts were lovely and perfect and pointed, and how I wanted mine to be whenever the day might come that they would appear.

'That's better,' she said. 'I was feeling too hot.' She came close so that she could see in my mouth. I stuck out my tongue and waggled it. She put her finger on my lip and pulled my mouth wider.

Taste the nectar, divinity, it is within inside every person and one can taste it and as soon as it drops into us, it just makes it beautiful, just makes it calm and cheerful.

'Are you ready, beautiful?' She was smiling, breasts close to me, her hair near my mouth.

'Yes, yes mmm.' It was hard to speak with my mouth open.

'Hang on, should I sterilize it, do you think?' It was a very pretty knife, it wasn't big or masculine, a sharp little pink knife.

'Nah, it's fine I bet.' I held out my tongue. She came in with the knife.

When the sting came, it made me clamp my mouth on her hand. We both screamed and blood ran over her fingers, down over my teeth.

I'd passed out and someone had put me in my room. My tongue was incredibly sore, and when I moved it around in my mouth I could tell there was crusty blood in there. I sat up. Someone had written a note and left it on the bed: GET THE FUCK OUT OR GIVE ME SOME MONEY. I had no money. My eyes were itchy and something else was coming over me, a feeling in my chest.

Finding it difficult to breathe, I went out into the hallway and knocked on the nearest door. It was a guy who hardly said anything. I'd tried not to speak to him the whole time I'd been there. He opened the door a crack and then a bit more.

'Have you got any change so I can go to the phone box?'

He shook his head. Then he raised his chin, looking at me. 'Not to give, but I can exchange, though.' I didn't know what he meant. I was touching my lip and my hurting tongue. I frowned. It was a little painful to speak. 'What?'

The guy opened the door a bit and gestured towards a heap of filthy-looking sheets on a single bed. His room smelled of old shoes, of cupboards under stairs. He was a small man, not much bigger than me, and bony-headed with bad teeth. He was speaking to me, but I couldn't make sense of what he was saying. My brain cells felt extremely grubby.

'What?'

'If you come in here and spend a bit of time with me there' – he pointed to the bed – 'then I'll give you some pennies to phone home, ET.'

Stepping away from him, I went back to my room. I looked around. The walls near the bed were covered in my writing. I had done it each night, and it was only now that I realized how much I'd written.

I ran downstairs; I wasn't sure what I was going to do. I stood in front of the door, thinking that if I went out, I might not come back. How could I pay Gaz anyway? I looked at the letters in a jumbled pile on the floor and noticed an envelope with my name on it. It had two letters inside, one from my mum and one from my dad. I didn't know how long they'd been there. The one from my mum was pages and pages long. I read the odd line.

I'm stoned while writing this, but that doesn't matter. You'll never know how much you've hurt me. I've been terrified. I've been waking up all night, and...

My dad's letter said: *I've left the job and I'm around the corner. I'm waiting for you until you're ready to come home. Dad.*

I opened the front door and ran to the end of the road. I went around the corner. There was the Beetle, but no one was in it. I stood next to it. One of Dave's old *Transformers* figures was on the floor in the back. A pack of rolling tobacco was on the dashboard. I tried the handle, but it was locked. I leaned against it. Closed my eyes. And then I heard his voice. 'Sue. Is that you?'

She was waiting in the kitchen, grim-faced and pale, thin, anxious, twitchy. I stood in the hall. She turned to me. 'I'm sorry, Sue,' Mum said. I'd never heard her apologize before.

'I can't stay here if he is here,' I said.

They nodded. 'He's gone.'

Dad made porridge, adding blobs of jam in the middle and stirring it to make it pink. I used to like it that way when I was little. They moved around me as if I was made of glass. After two or three days, I stopped blinking in my right eye, but my mouth was very sore. I had an infection under my tongue. Doctors, bed. They brought me Lucozade and antibiotics.

'You have to promise he's really gone,' I said. 'Or I will run away again.'

'We promise, Sue, we do.'

And it was the first time I saw that I could use words as weapons too.

Word Processor

I was frightened of the house I was drawing – or sometimes writing – and the way it crept into my dreams. My husband was going away on tour. This was normal: he is a musician, and separation is part of the rhythm of our life. But I hadn't told him about the gremlin-Maharaj Ji entity in my head that had been coming since returning from Crewe. Nor had I mentioned the never-ending drawings I was making and shoving in the suitcase. Nor the wall-writing in a spot behind the wardrobe.

As he dragged all his instruments towards the door and bellowed goodbye, I stood looking at him. I nearly stopped him to ask for help, but as I touched his shoulder he recoiled. He was preoccupied with leaving and then he was gone. As it had done since the children were babies, the house recalibrated without him.

The gremlin-Maharaj Ji only came when the children were asleep. At first, I walked around clearing away glasses and picking up bits of uniform and shoes. Settling, arranging and fussing at the house like fishermen with their nets. When it was very quiet, I felt their nearness, like someone sitting diagonally opposite the room on a chair reading a newspaper and letting their coffee go cold.

On one of those evenings, about ten at night, when I was unsettled by the company but trying to ignore it, I finally tried the number Tony had given me for Bill.

He answered straight away. I heard his laboured breathing. The slipperiness of the past was close. I tried to gauge from his voice what he looked like now. I imagined him wearing an old combat jumper and jeans and odd socks. His hair was white-grey and thin. His much older face had the hanging look of a person who has been through a stroke or a mini collapse of the soul. 'Are you the woman asking about the windows?' he said. 'The sash ones? They need replacing and I've been waiting, but apparently there has to be permission from the council, is that you?'

I did remember that voice. I held the sound of it my head. He had been in the fabric of my early years, every day, always around. Picking up, building, making, cooking. He had always been more well spoken than anyone else we knew. For a moment, I felt almost warm. That long-lost feeling.

Then I recalled other phrases. A hand through the brain fog – *want some acid, little Sue? See the world a little brighter?*

Did your dad tell you secrets? Are you good enough?

Could you ever be good enough to be given the secret?

Didn't anyone tell you, Suzy-Sue, that kids aren't allowed to come into the geodesic dome?

It's a place of bliss and wonder just for us grown-ups. Maybe one day, if you behave. It's up to me, did you know, when they get the Knowledge. They have to work for me until...

I stood up, agitated. 'I'm researching the Divine Light Mission,' I said. I explained that I'd been given his name. Would he be interested in talking to me about those years? I didn't mention my name or my parents. Like Colin, he didn't seem surprised by this phone call out of the blue. He gave a harsh and rattling coughing sound. Smoker's lungs.

'There are some insects I've noticed,' he said. 'I don't know what they are, but they are these weird things. Like, strange little tail bits and wings and antennae, you know, is it? Is it dust mites? I don't know, but I've seen them moving, look there.'

'I…' I didn't know what to say.

'There's a tiny crack, that's where they go, they slip in and out all night and that crack leads to my flat, inside, you know? I'd like to request that they be dealt with, along with my window.'

'Okay.' I said. 'I'm not from the… council or the landlord. I'm phoning about the… past.' There was a long pause. I felt ludicrous.

'You are phoning from the past? What do you mean, some kind of time travel?' He started to laugh, then it turned into a coughing fit. I looked at the notes I'd written on the pad of paper. I felt like an idiot.

You used pressuring techniques on them.

Every day for months, years, you worked on them, you told them they would get a secret prize, you told them it would all work out, you told them it would be perfect and beautiful if they did it all, all the things you believe in.

Do you remember me? John. Lynda. Others? You were very active.

Bill coughed more. The gremlin-Maharaj Ji in the room drew closer to me, amused, happy. I wanted to ask him why he'd targeted my parents, recruited them. Had he hung around factories, focused on people who'd dropped out of school? What had he got out of it? Had he been brainwashed? Did he regret it now?

I pictured Bill in a council flat with posters of David Icke and Illuminati eye-triangles painted on the ceiling with blood. Where do ageing hippies end up? Coughing, worrying about insects coming out of cracks. Then I thought of Tony, the heavy melancholia that emitted from him, and a sticky guilt washed over me. Why did I have to dredge up their pasts to stop the chaos in my own?

'You'll report it then, do something about it?' he said.

'Yes,' I said. 'I'll report the insects.'

'Thank you.'

I put the phone on the sofa next to me. I drank a small glass of water. I sat down and stared at the floorboards, attempting to join them together with the lines in my head. The screws in the wood constellated.

Are the kids safe? The question materialized in my head. Yes. In bed. Asleep.

'Do you remember me, Bill?' I said. 'Suzanne.' I listened to him breathing.

'No. Aren't you the woman about the silverfish?'

'No,' I said. 'That person wouldn't be calling at this time of night, would she?'

My voice had gone nasty, I could sense it. Bill coughed. I focused on the wooden floorboards. They moved slightly, began to contort. I squinted. I felt myself move, stand up from the sofa and lean forwards as if over an abyss. I was ready; I could tip inwards and go go go, as I felt something wanted me to. Was it the past? It was a tugging-down sensation. This was Bill, who had given psychedelics in the geodesic dome so long ago. Perhaps he'd done more: I understood as I heard him breathe that I would never know. There was a burnt-out patch that I could never believe, recover or understand.

I think I wrote it all out, a long time ago, back before laptops. I bought myself a word processor and typed it all and kept it on a little floppy disk that I have since lost. What did I say? I wonder. When words externalize there is a danger they will disappear and along with them the story they contain. I had always lived with a sense that a missing piece was just out of reach. It could have been blame. I heard the gremlin-Maharaj Ji clapping and cheering me. 'Yes yes yes,' it was saying. 'Go go go.'

'Go where?' I said to the room, but there was no answer. I felt panic flurrying in my stomach. I stood up. Picked some of the kids' stuff off the floor. School bags. A lone trainer. Then I was jolted back by my son's voice: 'Mum, Mum,' he was calling from the landing.

'Oh yes, hey,' I said.

'There's a really big spider in my room, it's freaking me out, it's near my bed. Can you get it?'

'Bill,' I said into the phone, 'I'm sorry, I have to go.' It had been such a long time since my son – big and ruddy and full of intense surges of testosterone and insecurity – had asked me to help with anything. 'Yes, coming,' I told him.

When I had sorted my son out, I flicked on the TV. Should I call Bill again? I debated with myself. A what? A reckoning. A remembering. Had he answered that he remembered who I was? No. I don't think he had.

It became important that I find my catalogue of lost items, right then, moving around my house, creeping across the landing, turning the bathroom light on and off, trying not to wake the kids, I couldn't find it. This was it, I realized. What I'd been working towards all this time: a level.

All the books and learning and reading and publishing and creating and manifesting and organizing and acute concentration and focus and thought and direction had taken analysis and time. Lots of time. It had taken a demon-driven fixation on the reaching of a level, and that level was a university – or similar space – possibly a university-museum, a big institution with a grand gate and an old sign and an archive of some description or other. I moved around my house. If I could just find my catalogue of lost items...

I said the words 'nest' and 'place' out loud.

Perhaps I could phone Bill again, now, and ask him why. Ask him for facts or truth, such as *Did you purposefully dismantle my family? And to what end?* But that man, talking about the insects, I don't think he would remember. My guess is that he would invent, obfuscate, misremember anyway. *Anyway. Everyone meditates, hadn't you noticed? What are you talking about?*

My phone pinged in the kitchen. I already knew it would be a message from Mum.

Bite bite bite. I answered my phone. I had guessed correctly. I said, 'I think I'm sick,' and she said, 'Oh no, okay, I'm coming over now.' Only that wasn't what she'd said. It was something else. She'd said, 'Will you come over now?' But we didn't hear one another. Perhaps she'd also said, 'I think I'm sick.'

I wished we had a significant, physical task to share. One that required no speech. For example carrying a coffin together. Holding it with our hands, decorating it with white flowers, gently placing it somewhere. A ritual that would take us beyond our spirals.

Houseshare, Early 2000s

Just as I moved to London for my shiny new job, my mum was thrown out of her flat in Eastbourne, but at the same time she got a position at the hospital in Brighton. 'You can stay in my old room,' I said.

So she moved into the room that was mine in a post-student houseshare in Brighton. A dingy seaside terrace with damp walls and transient humans all my age, not hers. She was forty-four. I was twenty-four. I moved into a houseshare in Brixton. A terrace tucked behind Coldharbour Lane.

It was heavy, carrying my Museum from university to my new houseshare. The National Express driver wasn't happy about putting it in the hold because he said the latches didn't look secure and he didn't want all my belongings flying everywhere. Also, he didn't want me to put the suitcase on the seat in the actual coach as it would take up too much space and it was too big to put on the luggage rack.

'What am I supposed to do with it then?'

He scowled, then dragged it up to the front and wedged it under the seat next to him. 'Bloody hell, that's heavy, what's in it?'

'My past,' I said.

He snorted. 'You're not old enough to have a past.'

I'd bought a ring-bound journalist-style notebook at the WH Smith at the station, thinking I would want to write lists to calm my brain, but my fingers didn't move. Instead, I put my head on the glass and cried, a light but unstoppable crying.

A man with a freckled face and very dark eyelashes turned from his seat and looked over at me. 'Are you okay?' He had an unfamiliar accent.

I put my hand to my chest. 'Yes, a bit of trouble breathing.'

'Can I sit with you?' he said. I nodded. I thought he meant on the seat opposite, to help with a possible asthma attack, but he sat right next to me. His thigh immediately rested against mine. He'd been visiting a friend, he said, and now was going up to London to change and then on to Manchester. He was French and his name was Pascal. 'Why are you crying?' he said in his nice accent. I was intermittently crying and trying to get oxygen into my lungs.

I didn't know. It sounded like nothing, and I could see that, in a way, it was nothing. He patted my knee. After he patted my knee, his hand stayed there. I didn't move it. By the time the coach was on the motorway we were kissing, and when we got to Victoria Coach Station, instead of going our respective ways, we spent forty-five minutes snogging in the doorway of a closed-down shop near the station.

'You taste of chewing gum,' he said.

'You taste of Bombay mix.'

He laughed. Then he pointed down at what I was wearing: a peach-coloured nightie as a dress, covered with a checked shirt, two pairs of black tights to thicken up my skinny legs, and Doc Marten boots. I had smudged eyeliner, my reddish hair was a matted heap on my head and I hadn't washed for a while. 'Why are you wearing underwear with no clothes on the top?'

'Boho,' I said, but I saw that the word meant nothing to him. 'Anyway, you don't seem to mind.' He was touching my breast through the fabric of the nightie.

'You are giving off a heat,' he said.

'Am I?' I cried more, thinking my eyeliner must be more smeared than smudged by now.

He pulled back. 'I meant it in a good way. You are very… hmm… fragile, perhaps?' As he said this, he put his hand under my nightie; it was only then that I remembered my suitcase.

It wasn't easy to flee from opportunistic and handsy Pascal, but eventually the urgency of my panic got through to him. He gave a very French bouf-ouf sort of sound, insisted I take his number and address in Manchester, and walked away while I ran around looking for Lost Property.

My suitcase was on the floor, but the woman insisted I describe it, then tell her exactly what was inside, to prove that it was mine. I said, 'Of course it's mine, I just told you. A brown, battered suitcase, very heavy, with a sticker saying MUSEUM on it.'

The Lost Property woman had dead eyes and a smoker's crêpe paper cheeks. She looked at me as if I meant less than a bit of paper on the bottom of her shoe, which I supposed I did.

'I need you to tell me one specific thing that is in this suitcase, so I know it's yours. 'That's the rules, you have to identify something.'

I tried to think: what had I put in there? 'Um, books. Papers.'

The woman bent down and began fiddling with the clasps.

'They're rusty and a bit fragile.' I remembered Pascal: *You are very… fragile, perhaps?*

She rattled and jabbed, finally pinging the clasps open, and then she opened the case so that the lid was facing me and she could see inside but I couldn't. 'Specific,' she said, leaning on the counter in a manner of monumental boredom.

'Please don't look in there, it's very private. You don't have any right to look in there.'

The woman went back to the suitcase and rummaged around in my stuff. 'Need something more spe-ci-fic,' she said.

'Diaries,' I screamed. 'Pictures of Maharaj Ji. Prayers to him, okay, prayers. Shit. Cassettes. I don't know. Notebooks. Fuck.'

She picked up a notebook, flipped it open. Read aloud: '*when I was born you were 16. I could be your wife. When I am older, I would like to be your wife. Guru play your flute for me. Perfect knowledge not…*'

I screamed and banged my hand on the Perspex screen between us. I started to hyperventilate. People in the concourse stared. 'Get out of my suitcase, get out.' I slammed my palm against the glass.

The dead-eyed woman slowly closed the lid, turned the suitcase on its side, dragged it to the door, opened it, shoved it towards me and closed the door again. I banged on the door. I heard the lock click.

When I turned towards the flow of people crossing the Victoria Station concourse, I saw a girl I recognized. It was Gemma from Crewe, a girl with black eyes and a knowing look and a savvy feel: someone who could withstand anything and had seen it all already. She was wearing boot-cut jeans and a black top, a scarf over half of her face, hair in a ponytail. She was moving at quite a lick, with a satchel across her body. She would help me now. Relief flushed through me, but I couldn't drag the suitcase towards her. I opened my mouth to shout, but the woman I had thought was a grown-up Gemma walked quickly past me. I understood that it couldn't have been her because she, like everything else, was gone.

Most lunchtimes I slipped out of my office for a cigarette on the fire escape. I worked on Portland Place, opposite the BBC building at the top of Oxford Street. I embraced office life fully. I wore pencil skirts and blouses, smiled at the South African security guard, sipped coffee and swapped comments with him about the bloody filthy weather.

How did I get here? I asked myself some days as my boots clicked through puddles on Northumberland Avenue, as I ran up the Portland Street office stairs, smiling at the bosses, shaking my umbrella. How indeed? Writing, studying, books and slogging.

My job was to organize things in different parts of the world to do with books, writers and translators. To begin with, I was in charge of organizing visas and paperwork, answering phones, checking budget sheets, hunting down staplers and rushing to get to the post in time. I slipped in and out of the lift, ate salad box lunches in the canteen, and let it be known that I was willing and able to hop on a plane at short notice. This was acknowledged by shadowy suited people from the 'Sixth Floor'. I zapped my identity card and hung up my coat. I was sent to a literature festival in Turin, a library project in Paris, a conference in Madrid, and before long I was visiting around two or three cities a month.

'Your pen is leaking,' the security guard said, and yes, I saw that I'd trailed ink all over the floor.

Soon, I had almost forgotten the old days. Soon, I was only about the new. I collected vintage pencils: Mitsubishi. Rotring. My compulsive writing was under control. I kept pencil cases, ballpoints and fountain pens to hand. But they were quiet, ruly, behaving themselves tidily in my office drawer.

I stopped mentioning to my parents the countries I was visiting. In blazers and boots with a satchel, heading off for meetings in Tallinn or Oslo, I got texts from either Mum or my friends in Brighton: *Your mum's cool. She can stay.* Or from my mum: *Your friends are nice. I'll only be here a while.*

At night, I swirled red wine in hollow glasses in cellar restaurants. I dissolved into whichever city I happened to be in. I belong here! I thought. On this terrace cafe, with a light breeze and delicious cheese plate. I belonged in the world and I could put aside the uncomfortable thought that my mum was between homes, between flats and semi-homeless.

My sleep was sometimes disturbed by dreams of the dredge of shingle on a south coast beach and I woke up shaking and sweating, but if I kept moving I could stay on track and afloat. Oh, keep me in a metro system. Keep me near the river. Keep me away from the sea. I began to steal things. Small items. A cheese knife from a restaurant in Sarajevo. An ashtray in the shape of a tiny whale with an open mouth from Madrid. It was this ashtray that I stashed under a window ledge up on the top of the fire escape at Portland Place.

There was a new security guard. One day he said, 'You shouldn't smoke, you know. It will hurt your lungs and look, this sky around us is already so dirty. You need to breathe.'

I agreed. 'I'm sorry you have to stand here all day,' I said. He had a weary look. He should have been retired. His skin was greyish and deeply creased.

'It's not your fault,' he said, 'but it is shit.'

I nodded. I leaned over the railings. From this vantage point of the fire escape at the back of the building, I could see right into a restaurant window. It was full of white men in navy-blue or grey suits and eating. My phone rang. It was my mum. For once, I answered it.

'Oh, you've bothered to answer me.' She was slurring. This was a recent development. Particularly after night shifts at the hospital.

I spoke quickly. 'Mum, Mum, someone else is calling me on the line, so I've got to go, okay?'

Snuffling noises, crying. I took a breath, a draining feeling coming through me.

'Are you okay?'

'I have to move out, though. I can't stay with your friends. I have to get another flat.'

'Okay, can we talk about it later?' I said. Then she began to speak fast, but I couldn't hear her words. 'What are you saying?'

'I was reading your stars... and it says... Jonathan Cainer, in the *Mail*, says it here, look... *it's easy to feel happy when things are going your way. The trick is to remain inspired in difficult situ... uations... that's where life stops being a game of chance and... becomes one... of... have to face adversity...*'

'Mum, I don't understand what you're talking about.'

'I met him, at a satsang. He is a great believer.'

'Who?' I turned my face away and into the light rain and wished that London would evaporate me, annihilate me, obliterate me.

'Jonathan Cainer, in the *Daily Mail*. He says someone close to you means you harm. Doesn't understand you and will fly... away with your soul.'

'Okay, Mum, I have to go, I have to go. I am going.'

At my desk, I pulled my expensive ergonomic chair forward and smiled at my colleagues. Later, I looked up Jonathan Cainer, the *Daily Mail* astrologer. There was an article by the journalist Francis Wheen about him: *This Cainer is a man who needs watching... he runs a website devoted to the cult.* Wheen mentioned that the Divine Light Mission had changed its name to Elan Vital. My phone pinged. It was another text from my mum: *HE SAYS YOU MEAN ME HARM.*

I sat in a meeting room underneath the fluorescent lights, looking at the wall of shiny green plants meant to bring oxygen into the corporate space. Everyone laughed at a risqué joke. It was raining outside, making it cosy in the office. I looked out at the trees of St James's Park. The offices had moved from Portland Place to St James's. We had a nice agenda to follow, marvellous. Minutes. Jostling, posturing. Business, any other?

A colleague said, 'Would you like some tea? Lemon and ginger? Green?'

I nodded, I smiled.

'Oatcake?'

'Yes please.'

In my Moleskine notebook, I wrote a list of to-dos as the meeting rolled on, everyone getting paid to talk in this room, nobody in a hurry. I calculated how many minutes of a hospital night shift my mum had to work to earn enough to buy one Moleskine notebook. I calculated how many hours of shift work at the hospital she had to do to pay for the boots I was wearing. Hot under my skin and itchy across the scalp, I wriggled on my chair.

I ate my lunch every day on a bench in St James's Park, reading Muriel Spark or Iris Murdoch or Penelope Fitzgerald. Novels about sitting on a bench in a park and being lonely in London.

I took the Victoria line each morning, squashed in and huffing with the other commuters. I embraced their church and wore signifiers of belonging and importance to differentiate me from pitiful tourists and visitors.

It was true that I was technically lonely. I hadn't lived with my housemates or worked with my colleagues long enough to know any of them properly. But it was a loneliness enmeshed with transition – shunting around the city or in and out of Europe – that I sort of liked.

Each day I zapped the security buzzer and entered the building in a spatter of rain. My desk was in the corner of a library full of filing cabinets with labels such as DORIS LESSING VISIT TO HUNGARY 1987.

My boss was the old-fashioned, gentlemanly sort. There were still a few of them drifting around literary London: smoked cigars, lunched with Graham Greene or Lawrence Durrell, once went to a party held by Robert Graves, got drunk with Peter Ackroyd. We discussed the shenanigans of the famous writers it was my job to offer international gigs to. *Don't put X on the same panel as Y. Keep Z away from the boys. Keep her away from him as he slept with the ex-wife.* In the archive stacks, I found a postcard with Ted Hughes's writing, spidery black ink, and I slipped it into my bag. There were reports on poets getting through the Iron Curtain in the pre-perestroika era. Notes from Diana Athill, Nicola Barker, Ali Smith. After a lifetime of reading, I was excited to meet 'real' writers until I quickly came to understand (as publishers have long known) that writers are human: moany, neurotic, sleazy, narcissistic and vulnerable. This was when I realized I hit most of those criteria.

I slipped from Gatwick and Heathrow on endless jaunts to elegant Gothic European cities – Krakow, Riga, Oslo, Athens – then I sloped back to the pubs in Soho or Westminster and down the crackling streets of Brixton, where I lived in a houseshare with an actor who read Proust all day.

'Would you like to travel here, there, everywhere, Suzy?' I'd changed my name to Suzy somewhere along the line and had worked hard to ditch Sue or Suzanne.

'Yes please. Let me run and keep running.'

I spun it out in hotel rooms, in lobbies, in meeting rooms, in canteens, in central London bars, with the light cutaways and the Westminster suits bustling in and crowding around each other pouring out gossip, and this way I blocked out the messages.

You. Sue. You mean me harm. I can't live here.

What can I do? Why don't you respond to my messages?

You are away. In those places, in those countries. I always knew you would go. They can see you, through you, to the accent that is the same as mine. How dare you move away from me? Where do you think you are going? Every word you write, every noise you make, every country you visit, every place you go, every book you read, every degree you get, every qualification you have, is a stab, with a knife, to my heart.

Compass

It took some persuading to convince the ladies of the museum to let us use the entire building rather than just the one room for my Museum of the Self.

I had explained my vision for a daughter–mother–grandmother–great-grandmother exhibition space. 'I'm going to film it,' I said. 'A sort of art project.' I hoped that people would walk around each area and engage with the sounds and artefacts in a contained way and also see how they linked together. I knew I sounded pretentious, but finally they agreed. I liked being immersed in this project. We were opening it up – for one day only, the next day – and we were allowed the evening to prepare.

My daughter's selection was laid out with great precision on a table near the window. There were four shoeboxes, each lined with thick wellington boot socks. Inside were small plastic items: unicorns, trolls, tiny pigs and miniature cats. There was a section of glass jam jars and inside each jar a specific item: a fake poo, a broken mermaid, a packet of magnetic dolls, kinetic sand, a fossilized scorpion, an owl necklace and a lead ornamental Border collie dog. My husband had set up a tape player at each 'station', and my daughter's nativity singing could be heard by putting on the headphones and pressing PLAY. I had told my son that it was the female line I was exploring.

My mum had given me the box of her stuff the week before. I spent ages arranging and rearranging her section along the edge of the stage. She had knitted a sign saying TREASURE. Grandkids' drawings. Teddies. Dolls. Various knitted items: seagull, bag, socks. Also a pair of wellies. Pyjamas, summer and winter. A jar of coffee. A geranium plant. Dreamcatcher. Tarot cards. The dog's bed. Tabu perfume. In the opposite corner was a tape player where the recording of her life that I had made over the last couple of weeks would play on a loop.

The museum woman was shocked when she saw the amount emerging from the boot of my car. Rolls of prints, art sketchbooks, a framed photograph of Gaston Bachelard's *The Poetics of Space*. A pot with a feather. A pile of Moleskine notebooks and then cheap notebooks stacked up and balanced so that they were taller than me. Paperweight, typewriter, Breton doll, cassettes, snow globes, an old word processor, drawing implements, fountain pens and old pencils, and a matryoshka doll.

I arranged them on the table and opted for no explanatory cards. I put a compass in the middle. I'd been teaching myself how to draw using a compass in the manner of the great master Hokusai. I hung up a small sign I'd drawn with Japanese ink: ALL THE LOST AND FRAGILE THINGS.

One of the museum ladies came towards me, frowning, as I was setting up. 'You know you agreed to just twenty-four hours? We have the bridge group on Monday.'

'Yes,' I said. 'I know. Thank you.'

'I have to go and do a meal delivery now to one of our older members. Can I leave you here, and I'll be back at nine to lock up?'

'Yes, of course, thank you.'

'Actually,' she said, smiling and patting my hand, 'you lock up, and open tomorrow? I'll be back on Monday. Please put the keys in the safety deposit box at the end of the day on Sunday.'

'Okay,' I said. 'Of course.'

I became somewhat obsessed with arrangement.

I moved things around, lined them up. A pair of ice skates I'd bought online. A kaleidoscope. It was a little spooky in the museum on my own. I shivered. I was wearing boots and a long cardigan and scarf, but still I was chilly. I spent a long time arranging the different cassette play-ers and my iPad speakers. I wanted the Maharaj Ji tapes to come out of the cassette player and overlap with the recording I'd made of my mum telling her story. I wanted the two to interact and overlay each other but not drown each other out. I wanted an exhibition for a day. Then everything would feel validated. I knew it was a whim. A massive vanity project and a temporary installation. But we had lost so much. The word *curation* means 'cure', and I had no other options.

I'd thought I would do it for Mum, to make her... what was the word? Validated?

I pulled my Museum suitcase to the middle of the room. I sat cross-legged next to it and felt like smoking a cigarette for the first time in years.

So many papers inside: endless drawings and lists. Was it true that if you kept walking and sketching, map-making, drawing, and using ink or tapping out ink via a screen or a computer, you would eventually find the way through?

I was talking aloud to myself. I thought of Vera Pragnell's dream and how it was all ruined by men. By her husband. And how museums are utopias, collections of things made into an arrangement of taste and suitability.

Running my finger along the edge of the lining in the suitcase, I searched for a slit made many years ago with a penknife – since lost, of course. I found it towards the right-hand edge of the case lid. I wiggled my finger inside. There was paper inside. I pulled out one sheet, then more. They were familiar, but I hadn't seen them for a long time, and it took me a second to understand what they were. Suicide notes my mum had left me throughout the years, dating back to when I was nine.

I love you. I am sorry. But I can't do it any more, they said mainly, or variations on those words. Later, they were copies of text messages that I'd written on Post-its. I had stopped doing that at some point; I wasn't sure when.

These notes were a part of my life, like a local street. I touched them gently and looked at the familiar handwriting. Individual words glowed out at me, cat eyes, then faded. I laid the letters out on the dusty, uneven floorboards. I spent some time arranging them in a row. Different-coloured paper, but mostly just ripped out of a lined jotter. I lay down next to them. I closed my eyes. My existence concertinaed in and out in a combination of hardness and softness.

I was in a trap, and everyone else in the world was free. The quality of light had changed. I always had a baby clamped on me and a toddler tugging at me. On nights when the babies couldn't breathe, settle or eat, Mum came and took them from me so that I could sleep. My daughter was clingier than my son had been, her mouth always open. She was a licking, biting, eating, kissing sort of baby. My body leaked milk, everyone was always crying, everything was liquid.

Even though the kids were small, I applied for writing residencies far from home. I pitched for travel-writing articles. I applied for bursaries to research books that took me to the other side of the globe. I travelled to Kashgar in China. To Myanmar. The second I got home, I planned a new opportunity to run away.

Everyone in the hospital calls her Grandma. She comes in the night when the babies are howling. She changes nappies and sings lullabies. She's the only one I can turn to when all the babies are crying. She always comes. I no longer call her Mum. We all call her Grandma.

*

I keep meeting myself in the mirror in the airport. That's where I find the other me. At the Clinique make-up stand, in the toilets, in the queue for a coffee, in the changing rooms, buying a last-minute summer dress. In airports, I transform into a slippery, shadowy version of myself. *Don't leave. Don't go. Where's the Sudocrem? Will you have the baby? Can you have the baby? Can you watch the baby for me?* I have to finish a book I'm writing – I have always been writing it, I can't seem to end it – and I have had no sleep. I am hallucinating as I shake hands and nod. Publishers are keen on the book, and I am invited to a dinner. And another one.

I have an eye infection I can't get a grip on and everything is in disarray. I am writing a book and going away, leaving the children behind again. Even though my daughter has chickenpox. I turn down a trip to India, where my book is coming out – India! China! Vietnam! – because it clashes with my son's first week of school. I sit in my garden and cry for an hour, proud of myself: I am a real mother.

In Beijing, on a research grant, away for a week, a woman I meet asks me about my children. I tell her I have a boy and a girl. Her eyes fill with tears. 'You are so blessed. That is such a blessing,' she says. I remember that women of my age lived through the Chinese one-child policy, and I take her hand and agree that I am blessed. I look at photographs of her daughter on her phone. 'Who is looking after your children now?' she asks. 'My mum,' I say.

*

I am on a train. My dinner consists of a bottle of water, a packet of sweets and some crisps. I am speaking at a book festival. I puke in the toilets and rearrange the first four pages of my novel backstage, scrawling across the pages of the published version. I travel to Segovia and leave the children behind with my mum. I drink so much Spanish wine that my vision turns grey. I travel to Huangshan Mountain to run a workshop with Chinese writers. I answer the phone and am told that my daughter has had an accident in the school toilet and that I must come in to clean it. 'I'm at the Yellow Mountain, in China,' I say, and in my hotel room I cry until I'm sick.

When I am home, my husband pushes a baby into my arms and goes on tour. We barely see each other. We cross in the night. When I return to our seaside terrace, I grab the babies and nuzzle and chew them and kiss them and hold them and squeeze them. Then, four seconds later, I feel a flat, cold, chilly sense of exhaustion, combined with tedium and a web of claustrophobia all over my body. There is nothing and no one I love more than my children. There is nothing that makes me feel deader inside than domesticity. My daughter waddles towards me with her arms up, wanting to climb me. I can't see out of my right eye; I have a recurring infection.

Everyone in the household is ill. It is love in the time of nappies. Calpol, sleeplessness and tantrums. There is no end. Domestic life swirls like a washing machine, and I slip in and out of my house as if sleepwalking. The book has sold well. The boundary between myself and my children is amorphous. My husband lurches past me in the hall, in the landing, blinking with exhaustion and oppression and love.

I sat up and rubbed my eyes. I was in the museum room. I had fallen asleep for a while next to a pile of Mum's notes. I touched one of them but tried not to read the words. Some were short, some longer. In a way, I supposed, they were love letters.

Remembering my plan, I looked around for the bamboo canes and string that I'd dragged in earlier. I'd been watching YouTube tutorials on how to build a basic geodesic dome with bamboo and paper. My husband had helped me cut the poles to the right sizes and I had the instructions with me. Still, it was confusing. I laid them out as triangles on the floor, tugged the knots to strengthen them. I had three false tries of raising it, the bamboo collapsing, but finally the dome contraption was up in the centre of the room. I walked around it in circles, tightening the edges.

Ideally, I would cover each triangle with paper, but I didn't have time for that. Instead, I tied string across each segment and then pulled out the old-fashioned dolly pegs I'd brought with me. I found it peaceful to be working on the assembly of the dome in the quiet evening space. I remembered Bill and Dad all those years ago, reading aloud to each other sections from the *Whole Earth Catalog*. Staring and poring over the 'how to make a geodesic dome' pages.

Over the next few hours, I arranged all the lost and broken things from our life around the dome. If a person had knocked on the door then and asked me to explain it exactly, what

I was doing, the whole endeavour might have fallen apart. But I moved on, solidly, diligently, constructing.

I thought: I've brought back all the broken lost things, and now it will be all right. I will reverse the curse and get rid of the gremlins and the badness.

If I were a quilter, I would stitch my mum's notes together into one bedspread. Or a kite, like the balloons stitched by people wanting to escape over the wall in Germany that my uncle had guarded with his guns, but this dome in this unsung place was the best I could do. What had she been thinking when she wrote each note? What thought process? What pain? I pulled out more of my drawings from the suitcase. Most of them were houses, or some variation of it. Nests or pods. Blueprints or aerial views.

I'd drawn square after square.

My eyes hurt. I wished I could swim. That's what I would like the most; water and stretching. I thought about inheritance and what it means when nobody, going back forever, owns land, houses or a sense of place. Each note pegged up *I'm sorry. I can't. It isn't possible…* I felt a dreamy sensation of moving backwards into rooms. Hotel rooms. Dream rooms. I remembered being in other cities. Beijing. Athens. Moscow. I'd spent a month in Moscow once. Staying in a hotel called the Cricket. It was modest and did not provide room service at night.

I often ate in the brightly lit restaurant at the Novotel, assuming a relative sort of safety in the big international zones. Russian salad of grated carrot and cabbage, fries and half a Spaten beer. I would order coffee and watch the flow of businessmen enter the lifts with impossibly tall, elegant women. I had started to work on what I vaguely thought might be a PhD proposal, or a novel, I wasn't yet sure. On one of these Novotel visits I picked up a glossy publication someone had left on the table and saw a picture of Maharaj Ji. I shivered and looked around me, half expecting him to be sitting in this bar.

He wore a suit. Underneath the photograph was the headline WORDS OF PEACE FOR EUROPE. The topic was the role that peace can have in individual and social life as a fundamental value. There were transcripts and photos from the European Parliament, an international conference in Brussels, and Mr Prem Rawat, as he was now called, was being introduced to the European Parliament as a 'prominent advocate for peace'. I read some of his speech: *Peace begins with every one of you. When you look at a city at night you see a whole area that is lit up. What you see is individual bulbs. These individuals need peace. They need to work on finding peace within them and it is on the individual being's stage that peace needs to dance.*

So he was still going, then. He still existed in the world. I looked him up on my phone as I finished my salad. He had thoroughly rebranded himself and had changed 'the Knowledge' to 'the Keys'. At least that's what Wikipedia told me. I felt a shift, a dislocation in a part of my brain, something behind my eye. I'd been reading about Katherine Mansfield's time in Paris under the Russian physician Manoukhin, who claimed to be able to cure her tuberculosis through the means of fifteen 'seances' that were, in fact, radiation blasts. I'd made the connection then, in that hotel room, between Maharaj Ji and the crank guru Gurdjieff, who had introduced Mansfield to something called 'Cosmic Anatomy and the Structure of the Ego', and I'd meant to bring it up and tell Mum about it, but I'd been jolted by a kerfuffle in the hotel. A suicide note had been left in one of the rooms and the place was swarming with Russian police.

I'd texted Mum: *Maharaj Ji is still going and did you know that Gurdjieff dyed sparrows with aniline and sold them as 'American canaries' in Samarkand?*

But how could I expect her to understand what I meant?

I pinned Mum's notes on string like cheerful bunting. Everything was ready. Like a snow globe, it was an offering of grief. It would make her whole.

There was a comfort to the motion of it. I felt something come together, a release. I was excited to show it and share it all. Make external the internal.

I walked in circles, filming the dome and Mum's notes and the houses I had drawn over the years. I'd filmed the various stages of its resurrection. The surprising sound of a siren made me jump. It was an incongruous noise from a cityscape that felt wrong in this village setting. I felt that I had been in hiding and that it had become harder to keep things under wraps and contained, but now – through this exposure of all the words and drawings – I could banish whatever was haunting me.

I remembered the Maharaj Ji-gremlins and their finger-nails tapping. I concentrated. Sat still. Listened. I wasn't sure, but at that moment anyway, I wasn't unnerved by them. It was when I was about to go, standing by the door and looking back into the museum room, that anxiety shot through my body. Would anyone understand this? But then, I thought, it didn't matter. It was for my mum and my daughter; they would know what it was. They would see through the stuff to the meaning inside. Luckily, I'd written and drawn enough by then to know that all attempts were versions of failure, and so this was my best.

I sampled the cassettes so that my mum's voice chimed with Maharaj Ji's in a playback loop. *So, our mind is very subtle... Bill was directly from the organization, high up, we met at someone's house... all the people's houses and then twice a year in a hotel room and make everyone smile...* I turned it off quickly. I believed it was all ready to undo the curse.

Exhibition

Everyone we knew was coming. It was a weird mishmash of friends and family, sort of like a wedding, and it was a bright, sunny day with snowdrops and daffodils in the museum garden.

'A pop-up what?' they said.

'Oh, just come, you'll see.'

Mum had invited some of the nurses from the hospital she used to work at, and they'd come in, enthusiastic, in a rush. 'It's nice to meet you, Sue, we've heard so much about you, your mum talks about you all the time...'

I squinted at this alternative version of my mum, popular with the consultants and trusted by everyone. Her ward sister had told me some years ago that she was extremely good at her job, excellent in a crisis, and that all the new doctors came to trust her. Professional Grandma was another species to me. She was chatting, spinning around happily, eyes bright, leaning over and laughing. No one had seen our exhibition yet; it was in the other room.

Dave and his little girls were in the corner with Dad, looking at the Vera Pragnell Sanctuary stuff in a glass cabinet.

Mum's friends moved in and out of the room, putting on the headphones. The tapes were playing. I stood listening. My mum's voice: *I was sad when it all started to disappear. They dropped off, got mortgages. John wanted to buy a house in Eastbourne, always wanted a bit more security. I said no. Hippies wouldn't believe in signing a piece of paper for twenty-five years. I did endless hours of slaving, but never for myself. No regrets about that. I feel like I had separate issues… people don't realize it because I have trouble with maths and understanding money, well, the hippy thing allowed me to be safe in rejecting all of that.*

I saw Mum disappear through the door with a couple of the nurses. I watched my daughter go in and out of the geodesic dome. She looked up, surrounded by the notes from my mum, and waved. I stood still, listening. I tuned into Maharaj Ji's familiar voice. *So, our mind is very, very subtle, very, very thin. So, this can only be conquered by those instruments which are spoken within us. That is, you cannot see the Divine Light with these eyes. You can only see the Divine Light with the third operation. That is the instrument, that is the operation. You cannot speak the Word, like you cannot speak the mind. That is the instrument to cut the mind. Now it is absolutely cleared away, done, completely finished. Once the mind is finished, the man is perfect and pure. Man is far-out. The man is completed. The surgery has been completed. The man has been made pure.*

I remembered Katherine Mansfield writing in a letter about 'doing operations on yourself'. I remembered Vera Pragnell writing about 'severing the part of yourself that cannot follow the Way'.

I had a vision of Mum falling off a bridge on to a railway track, smashing into a million pieces. I tensed. I'd been expecting it all my life, a phone call, a message, an official of some sort knocking on the door with bad news. I felt that if there couldn't be any retribution, any confrontation with Maharaj Ji or his organization or Bill or any of the followers, then this could at least provide a release.

Then I turned towards the table, where there were cakes and friends.

Later, I realized it had always been a battle for narrative truth. How many storytellers can you have in one family? I'm not sure there is room for more than one.

'This isn't right,' Mum said, 'the way this is arranged. The way you've presented it. This version of events. I think it should be different.' Her fingers scrabbled and scraped on the trestle table, grappling to reach one of the paper napkins.

I'd had my back to her, but my antennae fired up. I turned to see her lurch at the coffee table and stagger into it a little.

One of the nurse friends shouted from the door, 'We're off then!' And Mum spun around and shouted, 'Byeee.'

Dave materialized next to me. 'They snuck to the pub,' he said.

'Is that where they've been?'

They'd been gone nearly two hours. I glanced at my mother-in-law sitting on a chair near the sandwiches, talking to the ladies of the museum. I looked at my son, who was chatting to my dad. I put my hand to my eye and pressed it. My mum had been known to spiral after just one glass of wine.

'Why can't I get this working?' she said, pointing at Dave, jabbing a finger towards him and staring at the coffee urn. 'Dave, do it for me.' She slipped, pulling the paper tablecloth downwards away from the wall, lurching. A plate of biscuits slipped on to the floor.

'Mum?' I said, moving slowly towards her. 'Are you okay?'

'I've been in that corner, thinking,' she said. In a strange, dreamlike instant, something happened with the tape as it overlapped with her current voice. She was moving her mouth and speaking, but instead of hearing what she was saying, I heard her words on the tape. *Many people would be picked from the audience and a piece of paper came around and you were told when or if you were picked. We had to wait. Massive build-up, took two or three years. When it finally happened Maharaj Ji touched your head you feel like he looked at you deep in your eyes and soul. Bill said it opened chakras up. You had to run satsang meetings, there was an expectation and you had to pay a bit.* Then I heard her current voice. 'I know what you think, I know it—'

'Mum?'

'These things, representing everything I am not and everything you are...' She threw her arm out in a curve. 'You're all ashamed of me,' she said. She looked pale, and wild in the eyes.

'What do you mean, Mum? I'm not at all. I'm trying to explore and understand them. I did ask you. I did check if it was okay. When I recorded you. I told you about it, you said it was okay to play it. I couldn't understand my own story without exposing yours. You said yes.'

'Perhaps I don't have space for the wildness and the vastness of the amount you are ashamed of me,' she said, vivid, brightly fired.

I stood in front of her. 'I'm not, I'm really not,' I said.

Then a new sound came out clear and wild. I didn't see her mouth opening, but it was as if the words had projected out of her whole rather than formulating in the voice box, in the mouth. It was a stream of fucking fuck fecks and then another lurch along the side of the table. 'Dave,' she screamed. 'Don't ignore me.'

Dave put his hands over his face as if to defend himself from a thrown missile, and then he grabbed both his little girls and backed away. I looked over to Dad. He was also pressing himself against the wall. Everyone in the room was staring at us.

Then a calmness seemed to come down on her. 'Did you think that if you got all this stuff and put it together in a room it would make the past and the family better and whole?' she said.

I looked at her face; I was embarrassed. 'Yes,' I said. 'I suppose that's exactly what I thought.' I felt it then, the acute presence of the gremlin-Maharaj Ji. It was there. It was back, and I was frightened. Something odd happened to my vision. Mum's face was blotchy. My throat constricted and I felt as though I were a tiny child. My daughter emerged from the geodesic dome. I put my hand out towards her.

Mum swayed, and everyone was looking at us. 'You have that much faith in stuff that you bring it all here?' My daughter looked at her with wide eyes. I saw then that the gremlin-Maharaj ji had taken over her again, flitting all over her body and face. It rippled around her. I wanted to get my daughter, pull her hand and snatch her away, but I couldn't figure out how to get around my mum's swaying body.

Her head now morphed into Maharaj Ji's face and then shifted back to her own. I backed away from her. My palms were hot. I felt sick. She walked along the table and picked up the paperweight. She held it in her hands. Then she held it up in front of her face to look through it, like an eye through a hag stone.

'You think if you take this out of its factory or a little seaside shop like the ones I like and you put it in here, in this room, it will become what? What is it you are looking for, Sue?' Her voice was a sneer. It wasn't her voice, it was Maharaj Ji. 'Suzy-Sue? Something official?'

She started moving everything around. Putting the pieces of my stuff on the floor. Kicking things.

I remembered the cult specialist talking about the 'confluential trance', the place where people like my parents had stopped growing their autonomous selves to become part of the cult, self-identity-wise. When this happened, she had said, a pseudo-identity takes over. It is like a tumour, splitting the personality, blocking it, letting in another voice, another face, another identity. I watched her hold the paperweight. As she stood in front of me I fell through the wormhole in time, back to the garden in the 1980s, with Dad burning the photographs.

But I saw her take the glass paperweight (that was also a doll and a snow globe) and turn away from me, walking – where is it? A garden? Perhaps Bill's – and instead of coming to me she turned away, looking outside of the house into another blackened space. She became Nana, then me, then my daughter. We are a set of matryoshka dolls. I realized then that my greatest fear was to become her, or rather to destroy her, as we all do.

'Okay, okay, I see,' she shouted. 'I see, you are all here judging me. You are all looking at me and thinking you are better and that you know better, I can see that. Well, none of you understand,' she screamed.

My dad seemed to come out of a trance then and move towards her. I had a sense that ghosts were near, in the hall close by. The gremlin-Maharaj Ji was here. It was inside her, of her, through her, all around us, and was coming for me.

'Lynda,' my dad said, walking towards her, holding out his hand, but she had got hold of the coffee pot and knocked it over so that coffee was streaming everywhere.

She was crying. Every time my dad's hand came near to touch her arm or find her shoulder, she swore, making my daughter's and son's eyes pop out of their heads.

'Mum,' I said. 'I'm sorry, I'm so sorry, I thought I had I was I thought…'

The museum ladies, the friends, my husband's family gawped, mouths and eyes wide. Wasn't this what she had always dreaded? Complete exposure? Every person in the room staring at her. I knew then that I could never escape, that I was in a small, shut-up space turning left, right, left, right in a minuscule maze. Miscommunication. She thought I was trying to kill her. (Was I?)

She slid down the wall, crying. I thought of Bill's voice on the phone, talking about the insects coming out of the wall. I put my hand on my chest as I felt the claustrophobia of asthma rising. Here I was again, on a tree heading up to an attic. We only want a route through life, a little map, a way in and a way out, don't we? When there's no one left in the world who can be bothered to listen to us, what can we do but fire arrows at our children, who are saddled to us due to blood clots in an enamel bidet?

'Why will nobody listen to me?' Mum repeated.

I put my hands over my ears like a child. 'I've just recorded your story, I wanted to curate it, care for it, give it space... and you are... it's not working.' I was having trouble breathing. I couldn't hear her, but I also couldn't speak. She couldn't hear me either. I tried to remember if my inhaler was in my bag. I had been looking for gremlins and gurus to blame, but I couldn't exactly.

She was right, in that I'd thought putting everything in this place would create a harmony of some sort. I wanted to rehome the spinning things that I'd felt all my life that the Guru had stolen, or sometimes the mother/gremlin-Maharaj Ji had stolen, as it appeared to be merging into one entity. An arrangement of objects gives us the sense of cohesion, a utopian community.

I looked at her, disintegrating against the wall. I knew the theoretical contexts. I had discovered that meditation practices could have intense, adverse effects. I knew that there were so many words flying around. Alcoholism, profound depression, trauma. It was only as I glanced around the room at the terrible thing I'd done, exposure in the name of what – art? – that I knew all these words could just as well be applied to me. The endless writing myself out of a trap, an intense spin. I'd printed out information about a diagnosis I'd decided (with no training) applied to her. She scanned it angrily. 'You're telling me I'm a clusterfuck,' she'd said. God, I'd been presumptuous.

But also: I was desperate.

I scrabbled through my head, through the old tapes, through the old dreams and lies.

We have energy.

We have something that is realized in this lifetime, but it is scattered. We must bring it together.

Trust me. Come this way. Do this… the potency, the power of that energy brought together by Premies and our dream. We are special. This is real.

My daughter ran to me, held on to my knees and started to cry.

I'd researched all the words for it: 'discarding' or 'splitting'. She was in terrible pain, but it didn't help. It was the wiring of a shrunken amygdala and hippocampus in the brain. I was always trying to remember that. I stood up, pushed my daughter away and walked over to Mum as everyone watched. She flailed her arms around, trying to pull down the drawings of houses. Screwing up the pages, ripping them.

'Mum.' I took her arm and hauled her out of the room and into the side corridor.

We fell through the toilet door. I was the same as her; neither of us was the complete victim. She held on to the sink, looking at herself in the mirror for a second before looking at me. The door closed on heavy hinges behind us and I stood very close to her quivering face. 'I can't believe you've done it, this, in front of everyone, in front of the kids.'

Her eyes were red, and she was crying. I heard the confusion in her lungs, the wheeze and effort. I felt the same in myself. So much smoke in there. Then she twisted her head to look at me. 'You're so perfect. You are always so perfect. You do everything right, I'm just shit next to you, aren't I?' She was so angry with me her whole body was vibrating.

Tug my hair, would you? Move like that, would you?

A swing and tug, her foot on top of mine, crushing my toe. Move forward. Is she hitting me, or am I hitting her? Would we take skin from the face and pull it off? Would we stab if we had a knife? Would it be matricide or filicide?

I pushed her against the wall, she whimpered. 'There is nothing more I can say or give to you,' I shouted at her.

She slid down towards the floor. 'You never hear, you never listen,' she shouted.

'Every letter, book, paper, thing I've ever written has been for you…'

'I've read it all. I'm your biggest reader.'

Yellow-brown liquid seeped from a pipe underneath the sink. We were both on the floor. 'We can't go any lower, Mum,' I said, crying. I looked at her in the mirror.

Who was I fighting? Gremlins scampered over both of us, hopping around, enjoying themselves. Maharaj Ji's face shimmered a mask over hers and then disappeared again. The gremlins crawled everywhere, gleefully digging in nails.

I looked at myself in the mirror too. I looked like Mum from the old photographs, when she was young. We had the same face. The same masks. I was about to hit a woman in her late sixties with advanced lung disease who was already, in every way, falling apart. I was the monster.

'No shelter, no ashram, no peace.'

'Only pain.'

I'd come to understand that it would never, ever end.

There was a day, long ago now, when my daughter was a baby and Mum had taken her for a walk while I had a nap. I was tired. I had an eye infection and was exhausted from all the breastfeeding. I slept, then woke about four in the afternoon. My husband had taken my son out for a walk in the park. My breasts surged with milk; it was time for a feed. I felt like a machine at the mercy of others, a vessel for another human to exist. I made tea. I looked at the garden. Then I pinged Mum a message. No answer. I pinged another, and then I called. Her phone was off.

My husband came back with my son, who was a toddler at that point. 'Has she taken any milk?'

I looked in the fridge and two bottles of the expressed milk were gone. My breasts hurt now, so I had to squeeze out some milk. I turned to my husband. 'Where is she?'

He pretended all was normal. He was extremely calm in a crisis, always had been – he was anti-drama and downplayed emotions by nature – but even so, I could see a nervousness in his face. He drove around the streets of South London, where we lived at that time, looking for them. She was capable of strange, sideways things, unusual movements. It was as if there was something else controlling her, moving her.

I was anxious. I fed my son raspberries and gave him some water. I gave him bananas. I was tense and distracted as I read him his favourite Thomas story. I phoned Mum. I phoned my husband. He kept his voice relatively calm, but there was an edge.

She came back at 8 p.m. I'd expressed milk twice. She stood at the door, hair whipped and wild, one of her eyes watering. 'We had a nice day out!' she said. They'd gone on a little train ride and then come home. The trains had been delayed. Her phone had died. She didn't look directly at me.

I peeled the baby from her and went straight to the bedroom to feed. I was furious. If milk could be flooded with rage, then it would taste of green bile. I heard her voice; there was a cadence to it that I recognized. I couldn't bring myself to believe it was true. My husband came in to check we were okay. He rolled his eyes, but I could see he was angry too. He was keeping it calm. 'Has she been drinking?' I whispered. He didn't answer.

And yet there was another day, when the baby couldn't breathe, sleep or eat. My husband was away, and she came and stayed up all night, letting me sleep.

*

There was nothing in the museum that could make a difference. No possible arrangement that would contain our story. Space had collapsed, just as the Victorian British had scarred the world with their train tracks. I'd always thought I'd drawn houses or written to create homes. I thought of all my drawings of houses and scratched words. I now realized it was the train tracks that were killing the world and distorting everything.

'It's only by exhibiting like this that we become part of a community,' she said. Or I said. I looked at her. She is many things, but she is not stupid. She knew I wanted to assimilate her into the museum in order to elevate myself. (What to? I didn't know.) If I resurrected the burned photographs from all those years ago, would I drag Mum back out of the circle of fire, and myself too? I saw then that I had been trying to show her how to be... different. Less working class, more... supposedly palatable? I realized that she was totally within her rights to hate me.

'Would it feel better to you if I looked a certain way? Was able to be a certain way?' she said, reading my mind like she always could. Think of the museum signs teaching the workers: DON'T SPIT, WHISTLE, BE NOISY. This is the fold where the past meets the present. This is the point where one of us is victorious. It can't be both.

'Mum, if you carry on like this, if you behave like this, then you... you can't be... near the kids... or us... Or me,' I shouted at her.

Her face was white. She floated higher than the chairs; a thousand snakes came out of her forehead and her eyes swivelled around. 'I always knew… I always knew that one day you would say that to me. I've been waiting for it.' She went out into the cold air.

'You've forgotten your coat,' I shouted.

Fuck.

I sat shivering in the museum room. My dad was there, staring at the floor. 'I don't know what our battle is about, I think it's something primal, but we need some kind of intervention,' I said.

I waited to hear what he was going to say, but I understood that he had decided not to speak. What is the point of words and stories? There are too many storytellers in the female line of this family, and too many liars.

I lay down inside my recreated dome. It was still standing somehow. I don't know what I'd thought I was doing in recreating it.

I closed my eyes. The *Whole Earth Catalog* says of the dome and the nest: *The simple, organic construction makes the safest, most sound sanctuary.* I couldn't move from the floor of the little dome.

I remembered the first time I became aware of it.

I am six or so. Mum goes ahead with Dave. She holds his hand to cross the road. He is bright red in the face. I turn my head towards the wall of the Melts and see the bricks move and change. They rearrange in front of me, like mosaic squares I've seen in a picture book about Romans. They form Maharaj Ji's face. I hear the music brightly in my head. My new glasses are bothering me, and I push them up my nose. The wall seems as though it is leaning towards me. I understand with a bright clear truth that he – it, the shape in the wall, the Guru's face – is evil. Is bad. Means harm, and will kill us. It isn't that it doesn't care. Rather, it really, really cares.

It's raining, and they are at the edge of the road. A car splashes us. I feel the badness inside my mouth as if behind my teeth, as if stuffing itself down my throat. Mum steps into the road with Dave, and the bus is almost on them. I scream and she jumps back, hauling him towards the factory wall. They lean against it, panting. Dave starts crying and she turns to me and says, 'Oh, Sue. Oh, Sue, you saved our lives.'

SPRING

There is a glorious sun, not the sun that you see in the sky but a sun which is within ourselves, and which is much brighter, much, much, much brighter than the sun you see in the sky. The point of perfection is just all lighted up and waiting for us. We just go in there, peek our heads in there, and see it. It's just light and light and light and light and light and light and light.

Guru Maharaj Ji,
Speech to the Divine Light Mission, 1979

Seaside Terrace, 2020

We walk home from school thinking the sky is a strange colour. It's 20 March 2020, my son's twelfth birthday. It is also the first day the school is shut for lockdown. The kids are excited because it's unusual, and a bonus day off. They grab handfuls of privet hedge and throw them at each other. They run ahead and bundle into dogs and prams. I grab the children and herd them into the car. We're having a birthday picnic on the South Downs. Since the pandemic was announced I've had an intense need to breathe in countryside air. We climb up through a wooded slope called Church Hill; not many people know the paths up here.

'Breathe!' I command the children, like a madwoman. But the air is toxic, is it not? What are we to do with this new air? We look around for signs of a virus and try to understand what it means. My daughter wants to know what it looks like, what it does. My son wants to know if his maths homework will still be due on the same day, or has everything in his world changed? He's anxious. This is an abrupt shift and a collapse of the familiar. Will he speak to his teachers? Will he get detention? 'Of course not,' I say. 'The teachers will figure out a system. We'll all get there.'

Our path leads through a jumble of hawthorn, sycamore, ash, oak and beech. Bluebells are on the cusp. It's the tail end of the daffodils and primroses, and it seems to me that the trees have expanded. Their presence, always noble and impressive, has increased and deepened. I've been walking this area for over a decade. I know where to find a cluster of fig trees that will be dripping with fruit at the end of the summer. I know where the best conker tree is and the best patch for wild garlic. I'm on speaking terms with two horses called Rabbit and Friend who live in a triangular field at the part where the hill gets steep.

'What does lockdown mean?'

'I don't know,' I say. It helps to walk up here and breathe. We get to the top of the hill and eat our Co-op ready meal, sandwich, drink and crisps. The dog sniffs the air and barks at rabbit holes, creating an echo loop with himself.

Yesterday, desperately wondering how I was going to manage the enormous responsibility of homeschooling and working at the university at the same time, I printed off worksheets for the kids. One was an illustration of a lung's bronchial tree with the separate parts to be labelled: upper lobe, lingula, lower lobe.

My mum's texts have been getting increasingly panicked. They'd stopped for a long time but are now coming back.

I'm so scared.

And my dad, too. I'm going to isolate. The thought of dying by drowning in the air, not being able to breathe, is too horrible.

As we sit on the thistle-filled grass looking over at Cissbury Ring, my daughter asks me again what a virus is. I can see that facts will be helpful, so we look it up on my phone. 2019-nCoV. So freaky-looking, half alive, half not alive, strands of RNA floating-cosmic-particle-blobs with the power to bring the human world to a halt. What happens when they enter the lungs? she wants to know. 'They infect the respiratory tree,' I say. Mum sends a WhatsApp message: *I already miss the kids. They are my oxygen.*

We all three lay back on the grass, wanting to be part of it, dissolve into it or find protection in immersion. What I want, I think, is reassurance that comes from beyond humans.

A text pops up from my husband, saying he is joining us. My daughter sees him first, emerging from the woods, waving.

Four humans and the dog sit together, looking at the sky and the weird new world. My son springs to his feet. 'Let's keep going up.'

At the top of the hill, the path opens up from the beech tree tunnel. We emerge on to a grassy plateau. The sea in one direction and Chanctonbury Ring in the other.

We call the wooden seat up here the Queen's Bench. It does feel majestic to reach the top. My husband used to come up here as a little boy. 'Imagine,' we say. 'Little Daddy.'

'What's this bit called?' I ask him.

He shrugs. 'Dunno, it's just somewhere I've always walked. I don't know what it's called.'

When I look it up on an Ordnance Survey map, we discover that this place we thought was just an interlocking hill has a name. Surprisingly, but not surprisingly, it's called No Man's Land.

I'm outside a cafe in Eastbourne with my dad. The kids are running around tree trunks turned into an obstacle course. The sign on the gate says *Forest School Area*. It's the time of the pandemic, so we are socially distanced and can't hug. I offer him the page and my pencil.

My dad does the trick he's always done. The vanishing point. Start with a dot and then move outwards so the scene comes into view. Sketching, softly, lines around it. He managed to retire just before the pandemic, and he's tucked in at home with just enough to live on. His voice is light and his eyes are on the kids. I show him a wooden drawing box I've held on to all these years despite losing nearly everything else. 'Do you remember this?'

He picks it up. 'Jesus,' he says. 'I can't believe you've still got it.' He opens the lid and picks up a mechanical pencil, clicks its end and watches the tiny strip of lead stick out.

The kids run back to the table, grabbing cakes and covering their mouths with cream and chocolate. Even though my son is big with his cracking voice, and my daughter is slender as a bamboo shoot, they are still children. Red cheeks and sweaty hair.

My husband texts about dinner and the dog. Dad hands me back his drawing. It's a sketch of the park and the houses around the green spaces. He's caught the roofs of the buildings and the slant of the chimneys well. 'I like your drawing,' I say.

Dad shrugs off the compliment. 'Nah, rubbish.'

He hasn't drawn the virus, difficult weather or the world falling apart. But somehow, between his lines, in a way that can only be done in a drawing and not in words, he's captured the feel of the day.

I press my pencil into the page, doodling along the edge of his drawing, adding my marks to his. I write, I draw, I still have a burning sensation in my hands sometimes, but it feels different now.

'What are you thinking about, Sue?' Dad says, looking like his younger self.

I reach through the years to hold his hand, but I'm too old for that. I pat his hand for a second instead. 'Wondering how Mum is. Did she tell you her news?'

Catalogue of the Archive of the Museum of My Own Invention

I don't know how long we didn't speak for after the fight in the museum. We were back in the same cycle. It felt as if a shadow that had always hovered near us had finally landed.

When I spoke to a therapist, she said that the mind control business of the seventies didn't exist. It had been disproven. It was all tosh. Gremlins weren't controlling the mind. 'You have been looking for a ladder,' she said. 'A way out of the Melts, the factories, those places and those voices.'

Whatever happened that day with my mum changed something, but it didn't provide a ladder out in the way I'd hoped. True, I was no longer a child constantly running away from her and then compulsively coming back. But I also finally knew that I couldn't save her. The responsibility for her sadness lifted, bringing a new sensation of lightness. I finally let go of the compulsion to scratch, with ink, a tattoo-story into walls, paper and skin.

I put my hand against the wall in my hallway and ran my finger along the bannister. Our terrace, which had previously oppressed me, now felt warm and home-like. I set about thinking of a new exhibition. Both a book and a display. An arrangement of words next to drawings. I had been buying old blueprints of houses on eBay. I was working on a process of tracing the design on to the wood.

I'd used some money from writing to redesign the space in the attic. I didn't want to have a fear of attics any more, and had worked with my kids to get the space shaped outwards into something we could all share. A studio, with a skylight built into the roof. A desk area for us all, a reading corner and a huge bookcase. Drawing stuff and beanbags. I loved writing or drawing up there, and while I thought they would all stay downstairs on their devices, I found they drifted up and joined me. My daughter called it the Land of Ink.

Her text said: *Stage 3.*

So that means something like five years. But three have already gone. Or anyway, as it goes forward it must be managed.

She said, *I feel different about time now. The tiredness is enormous, pulling.*

I looked at the stuff I'd collected for years and realized only then that they were all variations on writing or drawing implements of one form or another. All different ways of scratching out marks.

It's late one night and my husband is away. The kids are in bed. I pull out my old Smith Corona. It's a beautiful typewriter, a light industrial blue. It's a Skyriter, compact. The original iPad. I put a piece of paper into it. My husband repaired it for me last year, got me a ribbon and brought it to life.

296 · THE MUSEUM OF LOST AND FRAGILE THINGS

Typewriter, ink, pencil, pen.

Dear Mr Maharaj Ji

Dear Prem Rawat

Dear Mr Rawat

Dear Mum, dear Mum. I love you.

Dear Diary

Can you bring back lost years?

Do you have regrets?

She tells me, 'Sue, I only have a few years to live.' And she says, 'I want to live I want to live I want to live.'

My brother's little ones are running around and I say, 'Yes, I come in peace. I come in peace.' The Missing Peace. Pieces of the fluttering notes, the suicide notes.

It's her birthday, and I give her my illustrated *Catalogue of the Archive of the Museum of My Own Invention*. 'It's all the things,' I say, 'that we lost along the way.'

RESOURCES

Mental health and families: www.mind.org.uk
Samaritans UK: www.samaritans.org, telephone 116 123
Family group support for drinking and alcohol related issues:
    www.al-anonuk.org.uk

GLOSSARY

Andy Capp   British comic strip created by Reg Smythe in 1957, published in the *Daily Mirror* and *Sunday Mirror* for many years. Andy Capp is a working-class figure who doesn't work and likes gambling.

beragon   The name given to a T-shaped prop for resting on when meditating, used by Divine Light Mission members in the 1970s and 1980s.

Burton's catalogue   Burton is an English retail company now subsumed into Boohoo.com. In the UK in the 1980s, the catalogue was used by people on relatively low incomes.

council house   A house owned by the local council and rented out at an affordable price to tenants, typically people who have lower than average incomes.

Crewe   A town in Cheshire, north-west England, known for its role in British railway and industrial factory heritage.

Divine Light Mission   An organization founded in 1960 by Guru Hans Ji Maharaj and later led by his youngest son, Prem Rawat. Scholars have noted links to Sant Mat movements (esoteric lineages with Hinduism and Sikhism), but the Western version of the Divine Light Mission is largely recognized as a New Religious Movement, 'cult' or charismatic alternative sect.

Hatha Yoga Pradipika   A fifteenth-century Sanskrit manual on yoga written by Svātmārāma, often studied within yoga teacher training programmes.

housing association flat   Housing association properties in the UK are residential properties owned by a private company and rented out to tenants who receive monetary help/subsidy or have accessed the property via the local council.

Provvy   A northern, working-class name for 'Provident Doorstep Loans'. The company stopped providing a 'home debt collection' service in 2021, after 140 years.

satsang   Sanskrit word for the practice of gathering for the performance of devotional activities.

Whole Earth Catalog   American counterculture magazine published by Stewart Brand between 1968 and 1998.

ACKNOWLEDGEMENTS

The biggest thank you goes to my parents, John and Lynda, and my brother, Dave. It's no fun having a writer as a daughter or sister, and you have been so understanding and kind about me putting this story out into the world. I am grateful.

Thank you to my agent, Rachel Calder, for editorial reads, patience and wise counsel over many years. The writing life can be rocky (understatement!), and working with you is a source of constant support. Thank you to my editor, Susie Nicklin, for believing in this project, for friendship, and extremely sensitive and intelligent editing.

Thank you to colleagues at the University of Chichester for helpful feedback, particularly Professor Hugh Dunkerley, Dr David Swann and Professor Hugo Frey, but also colleagues across the university. Thank you to students of my creative non-fiction and life-writing seminars: you continue to inspire me with your questions, brilliance and energy.

I wrote part of this book at the Heinrich Böll Cottage on Achill Island, Ireland, in 2022. Thank you to the Heinrich Böll Association for support and sanctuary. Thank you to the International Auto/Biography Association for community and events, and to Mary Stewart and Rob Perks at the British Library for awarding me the Goodison Fellowship in 2020–1, providing valuable research time. Thank you: Professor Catherine Loveday, Alison Moloney and Helen Barff for inspirational discussions around museums, memory and things.

Sincerest thank you to the author and manager of the 'Prem Rawat Bio' website (https://www.prem-rawat-bio.org/) and archive for permission to use vintage Divine Light Mission and Maharaj Ji/Prem Rawat images and quotes. Thank you to the Department of Special Collections, Stanford University Libraries, for the courtesy of allowing quotes from Stewart Brand's *Whole Earth Catalog*. Thank you to Professor Miguel Farias for advice on (the lack of) data regarding the impact of meditation and psychedelic practices on children. Thank you, Dr Gillie Jenkinson, for advice regarding therapeutic recovery for victims of multigenerational thought-reform influences, and a special thank you to Nick Lowe, who took the time to share his experience performing at Glastonbury in 1971 (before he was rudely interrupted).

Thank you: Helena Rebecca Howe, Alice Khimasia, Cathy Byrne, Tanya Andrews, Jonathan Barker, David Parr, Stephanie Burke, Laila Hourani, Emma House, Lydia Bell and Tamera Howard. Thank you: Woody and Scout, and above all, Ben Nicholls.

Transforming a manuscript into the book you hold in your hands is a group project.

Suzanne Joinson would like to thank everyone who helped to publish this book:

THE INDIGO PRESS TEAM
Susie Nicklin
Phoebe Barker
Michelle O'Neill

JACKET DESIGN
Luke Bird
Ben Nicholls

PUBLICITY
Karen Duffy

TRANSLATION RIGHTS
The Marsh Agency Ltd.

EDITORIAL PRODUCTION
Tetragon

COPY-EDITOR
Sarah Terry

PROOFREADER
Alex Middleton

THE
INDIGO
PRESS

The Indigo Press is an independent publisher of contemporary fiction and non-fiction, based in London. Guided by a spirit of internationalism, feminism and social justice, we publish books to make readers see the world afresh, question their behaviour and beliefs, and imagine a better future.

Browse our books and sign up to our newsletter for special offers and discounts:

theindigopress.com

Follow *The Indigo Press* on social media for the latest news, events and more:

🅧 @PressIndigoThe
🅞 @TheIndigoPress
🅕 @TheIndigoPress
🅞 The Indigo Press
🅙 @theindigopress